MW00576246

Allies

for

Awakening

Also by Ralph Metzner

The Toad and the Jaguar (2013)
The Ecology of Consciousness 7 vols. (2008-2013)
  1 *The Expansion of Consciousness*
  2 *The Roots of War and Domination*
  3 *Alchemical Divination*
  4 *MindSpace and TimeStream*
  5 *The Life Cycle of the Human Soul*
  6 *Six Pathways of Destiny*
  7 *Worlds Within and Worlds Beyond*
Eye of the Seeress – Voice of the Poet (2011) German/English poem translations
Birth of a Psychedelic Culture (2010) with Ram Dass & Gary Bravo
Sacred Vine of Spirits – Ayahuasca (ed. 2006)
Sacred Mushroom of Visions – Teonanácatl (ed. 2005)
Green Psychology (1999)
The Unfolding Self (1998)
The Well of Remembrance (1994)
Through the Gateway of the Heart (ed. 1985)
Know Your Type (1979)
Maps of Consciousness (1971)
The Ecstatic Adventure (ed. 1968)
The Psychedelic Experience (1964) with Timothy Leary & Richard Alpert

CDs
Spirit Soundings (2012) Poems, with music by Kit Walker
Bardo Blues (2005) Songs with Piano

Allies

for

Awakening

Guidelines for productive and safe experiences with entheogens

Ralph Metzner

Green Earth Foundation
&
Regent Press

Copyright ©2015 by Ralph Metzner

ISBN-13: 978-1-58790-308-3
ISBN-10: 1-58790-308-3
Library of Congress Control Number: 2015931137

Cover Illustration
Alchemical Emblem (from *Atalanta Fugiens, 1618)* decoded as *purificatio* practice.
From: *Worlds Within and Worlds Beyond* by Ralph Metzner *(2013, p. 87.)*

Layout and Design
Cynthia Smith

Published by
REGENT PRESS
www.regentpress.net
for
GREEN EARTH FOUNDATION
www.greenearthfound.org

Printed in the U.S.A.
REGENT PRESS
2747 Regent Street
Berkeley, CA 94705
e-mail: regentpress@mindspring.com

Printed on recycled paper

At these times of renewal of life on Earth, new designs, new life, and new tribes are being animated. We who are here now are being invited to come closer to the center and take a look at what's happening there. We are invited to come closer to the heart, where colorful seeds of life are germinating and radiant designs are looking for a path to manifest their physical existence.

Arkan Lushwala

The Time of the Black Jaguar

2012

Contents

Introduction

The drugs and plants in the general class of mind-altering or consciousness-expanding substances, which are known to have profound effects on the language centers in the brain, also have led to a curious set of terminological debates among researchers. No one seems to agree on what to call them! The classic triad of LSD, mescaline and psilocybin were called *psychotomimetic* ("psychosis-mimicking," although they don't, except sometimes), *hallucinogenic* ("hallucination-inducing," although they don't, except sometimes), *psychodysleptic* ("painful experience producing," although they don't, except sometimes), *psychedelic* ("mind-manifesting," although they don't, except sometimes) and *entheogenic* ("inner divinity connecting," although they don't, except sometimes).

The research with psychedelic drugs carried out during the 1960's by the Harvard group around Timothy Leary and others in other centers, led to the hypothesis, now widely accepted by medical and scientific researchers in the field, that these substances should be considered *nonspecific awareness amplifiers*. Unlike all other mood- or mind-altering drugs, including stimulants, depressants, tranquilizers and opiates, the actual content of a psychedelic experience can only be understood and/or explained by considering the "set" (intention, preparation, attitude, and personality) and the "setting" (physical and social context, presence and attitude of others, such as friend, guide or therapist). The actual drug (whether synthesized chemical, or plant or fungal preparation) functions as a kind of catalyst for perceptual, emotional and mental changes that can lead to insight, healing, learning, visions and delight – or they may trigger confusion, anxiety, paranoia, delusion and depression.

With these substances, both positive and negative states, the good trips and the bad, will tend to be experienced with amplified intensity and elaborate detail. If the set and setting is one that is supportive, therapeutic and protected, people will often say that they learn as much from the so-called "bad trips" as the good. A bad trip, in other words, may have parts that are subjectively painful and uncomfortable, but still, in retrospect, people will often say they learned valuable lessons.

This may in fact be one key to distinguishing mind-expanding substances and experiences from purely recreational drug experiences. In *Worlds Within and Worlds Beyond* I describe intentional guided entheogenic journeys to both heaven and hell worlds, as well as the four other worlds in the Buddhist cartography of the *Wheel of Birth and Death*. Many people reported that while they found the heaven worlds pleasing and beautiful, they learned more from the hell worlds – including of course, the essential lessons on methods for getting out of hellish states of consciousness.

In my own thinking and writings on this class of drugs I have, in recent years, come to avoid the use of the term psychedelic, which was coined by Aldous Huxley and Humphrey Osmond in the early 1960s, mostly because the term has accrued all kinds of excess cultural baggage – of illegality, danger, madness – which it didn't have at first. This was brought home to me when my 9-year-old daughter came home from school one day and delightedly referred to some paisley pattern designs she saw somewhere as "ooh, ooh, how psychedelic." Obviously, a descriptive term for certain class of drug experiences had morphed into a pop-cultural fashion image. Synchronistically, around that time I came across some early correspondence between Tim Leary and Albert Hofmann, in which the latter expressed his delight at the concept and terminology of "consciousness expansion."

I have also come to prefer that term now because it uses two everyday well-known words – "consciousness" and "expansion" and puts them in a new juxtaposition. It's as if one were to say "consciousness can expand – who knew?" And that question could then lead one to consider the parallel question about "consciousness contraction," which covers both the functional and intentional contractions of concentration and focus as well as the dysfunctional inadvertent contractions of obsessions and addictions. This line of thought then leads to one of the main areas of therapeutic application of consciousness-expanding (CE) drugs – namely in the therapeutic treatment of addictions, obsessions and compulsions.

In my book *MindSpace and TimeStream*, I argue that our states of awareness or consciousness fluctuate daily and even hourly between more expansive and more concentrated modes. Some of these state changes are intentional and purposive, while many others are involuntary and without accompanying recognition or insight. As is well known, one of the main purposes or functions of mindfulness meditation practice is to bring the more or less random movements of the mind and attention under some degree of volitional control. Conversely, one of the main functions of psychotherapy is to bring the involuntary contractions of obsessions and compulsions, mental, emotional and behavioral, under greater intentional control. *are they different?*

The term *entheogenic*, which emerged into use during the 1980s, in part as a defense against the pop-culture associations of "psychedelic," is the only one among the above labels that refers explicitly to the capacity of these experiences, given favorable conditions of set and setting, to put one in touch with the sacred or divine dimensions of our existence. Scientific studies have shown that given favorable conditions of set and setting, these substances can aid and support healing or psychotherapy; they can function as allies in overcoming addictions and compulsions; they can assist those who are dying in their preparations for the final passage; they can further understanding of states and dimensions of consciousness and the nature of reality; they can enhance creativity – and they can increase the openness to and likelihood of spiritual or mystical experience.

In this book I will be discussing the uses and values of entheogenic or consciousness expanding substances in sessions where the explicit intention or purpose, expressed in the arrangements of set and setting, is *therapeutic or healing, spiritual or sacramental, exploration or increased understanding*, and *enhancement of creativity*. This means I am not considering or describing the experiences of those who are using these substances primarily for recreational purpose – as in rave dancing or party environments.

Not that I am passing any judgments on the recreational uses of psychedelic (as long as they are done safely and with ethical consideration of others) – indeed I have enjoyed those kinds of experiences myself on occasion. However, the recreational use of mind-expanding substances does not really require any guide books or special training besides ordinary and informed common sense. Of course, recreational enjoyment may indeed be one motivational factor among others in the kinds of set and setting contexts I am describing. After all, in its essential root meaning *recreation* refers to a process of "re-creating" – which can itself be considered an aspect of healing.

Expansion of consciousness, or *magnification of perception*, or *awakening of awareness*, are all phrases that are suggestive of the non-specific content of experiences with these substances. Tim Leary used to point to the analogies of psychedelics with the microscope and telescope as scientific tools for the amplification and magnification of perception. What we see through the microscope is a function of what we put on the slide to look at and what we see through the telescope is a function of the part of the sky toward which it is oriented. The perceptual instruments allow us to observe phenomena at a scale or reality to which we don't have access in our ordinary functional waking state. Similarly, intentional entheogenic experiences allow us to perceive our psychic contents with a degree of amplification and understanding ordinarily difficult to attain.

Expansions of consciousness can and do occur naturally and spontaneously in the course of everyday life – when we wake up after sleep, when we travel and explore some area with interest and curiosity, or when engaged in mindful meditation, erotic communion or aesthetic contemplation. The ultimate expanded state is the "cosmic consciousness," or mystical oneness with the Divine – an ineffable, transcendent state in which all separateness is dissolved. Like all states of consciousness, such states are transient, though the understanding and serenity gained may stay with us for a lifetime.

In the famous Good Friday study on "experimental mysticism," conducted in the course of the Harvard research studies with psilocybin in the late 1960s, Walter Pahnke had demonstrated that when a group of theology students with an interest in religious experience were given a consciousness-expanding substance in a religious ceremonial setting, a significantly high percentage had classical mystical experiences. When Charles Tart interviewed several long-term practitioners of Buddhist meditation, asking them about their use of LSD and other psychedelics, most of them stated that while they did not use drugs regularly, their psychedelic experiences did play a significant role at the initiation of their practice – providing them with an inspiring preview of what was possible.

The experience and process of consciousness expansion may be more fully appreciated by contrasting it with *consciousness contraction*. The prototypical contraction of awareness is *concentration* and *focus*: when I narrow the scope of attention on some object of sense perception (what I'm seeing or hearing) or on some skilled expressive or executive performance (what I'm doing or making), I am thereby excluding more peripheral elements of potential experience. We are constantly modulating the scope of perceptual focus, widening and narrowing according to our intentions and the requirements of the situation.

In the course of ordinary life our attention and awareness is often drawn to particularly insistent or prominent (i.e. loud or bright) stimuli. Or we may be captivated by the attractive appearance of an individual or a work of art. In meditative practice, the motionless and eyes-closed position facilitates both the detachment from the compelling sense stimuli of the external world and the inward-turning of attention toward our own thoughts, images, feelings and sensations.

Whereas intentional concentrative contraction of awareness is essential to all learning, creative expression, skilled performance and effective communication, involuntary contractions of consciousness occur in states of fear and rage, where the narrowed eyes, adrenal activation and tensed up muscles ready the organism for the flight-or-fight reaction to a perceived threat. Such escape, avoid or attack reactions may become conditioned into repetitive fixations – and develop into the obsessions, compulsions and addictions that Sigmund Freud called the "discontents of civilization."

In the 20th century and beyond, we have been seeing the slow and halting emergence of human population groups from ethnocentric, tribal and nationalist identifications to increasing identification with the global family of man – a sense of belonging with this planet, this Earth, and a sense of responsibility for all humans, regardless of ethnicity or nationality or religion. At the same time, the ecology movements have made us aware of the limitations of our human-centered, human-superior attitudes, what some have called the "arrogance of humanism," and the disastrous consequences of this humanist arrogance for all non-human life. Our worldviews need to expand to become eco-centric and biospheric – so that we care equally for the preservation of all life on this planet, human and non-human. This is the shift that is needed if our civilization is to survive the impending collapse of the planetary environment.

In the worldview changes now taking place, we hear a lot about globalization – but this refers usually to the globalization of markets and profits for multinational corporate cartels. What we need more urgently for the well-being of our planetary civilization is a globalizing circle of caring and compassion, in which all of us take responsibility for all of us. Eventually we may develop a conception of ourselves as living with myriad billions of other human and non-human beings on Earth, in a vaster cosmos teeming with likely inhabited planetary worlds and civilizations.

Entheogenesis means the awakening realization that we human beings and the world around us are much more than simply material organisms living and evolving on a material planetary body. We are multi-dimensional spiritual, cosmic, noetic, psychic and earthly beings. The Sufi mystics offered the analogy that we humans are the occupants of a multi-storied mansion, but have focused our attention and awareness for so long on the ground floor, that we have forgotten even the existence of the higher levels, much less the methods of accessing them. In the Eastern religious worldviews, such as those associated with Hinduism and Buddhism, the existence and reality of higher, spiritual dimensions of our being is accepted as a matter of course, and many different yogic methods of meditation developed to access them. The central consciousness-expanding insight that emerges from psychedelic, entheogenic states and is confirmed by the perennial spiritual traditions of East and West, is that at every level, from macro-cosmic to the micro-cosmic, from atoms and animals, to trees and planets and stars, Spirit dwells within created forms and expresses through them.

Setting and ethics for entheogenic experiences

Generally, the preferred setting for sessions in the therapeutic-sacramental mode is a serene, simple, comfortable room in which the subject, client, or voyager can recline or lie down and the therapist or guide can sit nearby. Clothes should be loose and comfortable, and a blanket should be available in case of transient episodes of chilling.

It is best if there is access or proximity to the elements of nature. A fire in the fireplace serves as a reminder of the alchemical fires of inner purification and the life-preserving fire of Spirit. Fresh water to drink and proximity to a stream or ocean reminds us of the watery origins of our life. Earth and its natural forms — soil, plants, trees, rocks, wood — should also ideally be close to the touch. Trees or plants in or near the room of the session make wonderful companions. Crystals or other beautiful stones may be brought and contemplated.

There are two general principles that could be proposed as ethical guidelines for this kind of practice – and that are in fact widely supported in the underground entheogenic culture.

(1). No one should be given the substance, or be persuaded to take it, against his own wishes or without full disclosure of possible risks and benefits. An obvious corollary of this principle is that under-age juveniles, who are assumed to be less capable of making informed judgments, should not be induced to take these substances.

(2) No one should consider providing a session to others with these substances who has not had personal experience, preferably repeated.

The questions, purposes, or agenda brought to the session, as we will describe in detail in this book, basically set the tone of the experience. Whatever unfolds during the experience seems to be, in a sense, an answer to those questions— even though this may not become apparent until later. Most therapists and guides suggest to the voyager to first go deeply within, to the core or ground of being, to the Higher Self — or similar directions. From this place of being centered, with compassion and insight, one can then review and analyze the problems and questions of one's life that one brings to the experience. It is not uncommon for people to feel and report to the therapist that all their questions and problems have been dissolved in the all-embracing love and compassion that they are feeling. Even with such an initial state of total unity and transcendence, it is often helpful later to ask the questions, and perhaps record one's answers or comments, on tape for post-session review.

A final comment about the sub-title of this book – *Guidelines for productive and safe experiences with entheogens.* I am deliberately not using the term "effective," because to say an experience with a substance or method is effective implies the existence of some kind of standard of effectiveness that is being measured. This may indeed be appropriate when we are assessing a method of treatment for a defined condition of illness. We may ask "how effective is the cure?" But when we are talking about awakening and expanding awareness into previously unknown and unmeasured areas of health, well-being, creativity and spirituality – then the evaluation would need to be in terms of how productive is the new method? How productive of new forms of creativity, healthier approaches to the issues of living in these times in this world, new understandings of ultimate mysteries of death and beyond?

One

Intention and Preparation

The mind is at every state a theater of simultaneous possibilities.
My experience is what I agree – or choose – to attend to.

~William James

In this part I will describe and discuss the all-important factors of intention, set and setting and preparation for the most commonly encountered situations involving entheogens/psychedelics. As mentioned in the introduction, the kinds of sessions I will describe will be limited to those where the primary purposes are therapeutic or healing, spiritual or sacramental, exploration/understanding and the enhancement of creativity. I will not describe those kinds of sessions in which the primary purpose is recreational (e.g. rave dances) – although spontaneous pleasure, humor and delight may of course be aspects of any entheogenic experience. I will describe psychotherapeutic sessions in medical or non-medical contexts as well as ceremonies within the context of a more or less tightly organized religious framework. In the longest section I will describe the key elements of the hybrid entheogenic group ceremonies that have arisen in Europe and North America in the past twenty to thirty years. These ceremonies, which are extremely diverse in their detailed practices, draw on the shamanic and spiritual-religious traditions as well as psychological insights coming out of modern psychotherapy and consciousness research. I emphasize that I am describing these practices as an ethno-psychologist in participant-observer mode. I describe but do not advocate the use of any entheogenic substances by anyone.

Psychotherapeutic individual sessions in a medical clinic

These are typically held in a clinical research-oriented environment, with medical safety back-up facilities. Intentions are usually two-fold: *one*, to treat certain specified conditions, such as PTSD or anxiety and *two*, to test or demonstrate the value and safety of a particular treatment protocol. Examples of this paradigm are Stanislav Grof's work with psycholytic therapy in Prague in 1950s and at Spring Grove Hospital in Maryland; the work of Michael and Annie Mithoefer, testing MDMA-therapy with traumatized veterans. Although the sessions are conducted in a medical/clinical setting, the actual session room is typically furnished like a comfortable living room, with art and flowers. There are usually several psychotherapy or counseling sessions beforehand, exploring the issues involved, before the psychedelic or empathogenic session. During the session, which may involve the client staying over night at the clinic, the individual is listening to chosen music with headphones provided. The therapist, or at best two therapists, male and female, may interact with the client providing varying levels of psychotherapeutic support or guidance.

A variant of this model is the set-up for narcotic *drug addiction treatments* with *ibogaine* – for which several clinics exist - in Canada, Netherlands, Mexico and Guatemala. Because of the risk of cardiac collapse in the population of addicts during withdrawal and because the dosages of ibogaine administered are extremely high to counter the narcotic drug effect, these are high-risk treatments that have to be administered in fully equipped medical emergency rooms, with constant staff monitoring. The patient themselves are usually pursuing their own inner self-analytic process, with consultation available over the course of the session which may last 5-7 hours and require one to three days stay in or near the clinic.

Growth-oriented sessions in a non-medical group context

A group of six to ten individuals meet together in a living-room environment, at the invitation of a guide or sponsor. Different substances, including MDMA, LSD, mushrooms and others may be offered to choose from. The overall shared and assumed purpose is self-directed healing and personal growth, although these may or may not be explicitly described or discussed. Similarly, there may be varying levels of explicit spiritual or religious leanings – although these also are not necessarily shared. Certain ground rules about safety are stated and agreed. The group leader or host may offer an introductory prayer, such as from *The Course in Miracles*. Participants arrange themselves comfortably on mats on the floor, sometimes in a circle or sometimes not, with individual headphones providing music from a central source. There is little or no interaction among the participants during the session, nor is verbal guidance provided by the sitters – though they are available to offer support when requested. Participants are expected to take complete responsibility for their own inner work on their questions and intentions.

A variation of this format is provided by the group sessions Alexander "Sasha" Shulgin used in the research exploring newly created drugs, as described in the books *PIHKAL* and *TIHKAL*, co-authored by Sasha and Ann Shulgin. In these groups only one specific substance was ingested by all the participants in each session and the purpose was to evaluate a new compound that Shulgin had created. He and a constant group of about a dozen research associates would meet together in a familiar living-room environment, establish a safe dosage range and evaluate each substance on a five-point scale of subjective intensity. If we consider the effects of psychedelic compounds to be a function of (1) the substance, (2) the set and (3) the setting, his research method holds the set and setting constant, which allowed for meaningful comparisons between different substances. His setting was a comfortable home, in which people could move among different rooms and meet together to rate each compound tested and describe its effects. Certain rules of etiquette were agreed to by all, precautions and procedural signals established, so that any participant could veto any aspect of the situation with which they were uncomfortable.

Traditional peyote ceremony of the Native American Church

The ceremonies of the NAC are usually held at the request of a family or individual who are seeking healing or peace-making for some condition – such as an illness or behavior problem in the family. Someone agrees to sponsor the ceremony, provide a place for the tipi, invite a recognized elder to conduct the ceremony, purchase and provide the medicine cacti and send out invitations to potential participants. Different groups within the NAC may differ considerably on the selection criteria for participation – some of the more conservative groups may include only those with at least 50% Native American genes, i.e. at least one "native" parent.

One of the strengths of the traditional ceremonies, based more or less on the NAC model, is the time devoted to preparation.

I've attended several of these "meetings," as they call them. People were invited to assemble at the specified location and then slowly gathered over the space of several hours, with no starting time specified for the ceremony. The *Roadman* and his associates were said to be on "Indian time." A tipi was erected, wood for the fire assembled and stacked and meticulous attention paid to constructing the "altar" between the Roadman's seat and the fire-site in the center. Fine sand is brought in and shaped into a curved bank of sand, about six inches high, in the shape of a half-moon, between the Roadman's seat and the central fire. I once observed a couple of young assistants or apprentices spend several hours shaping and cleaning and smoothing the half-moon altar, using soft paintbrushes – while people were gradually assembling outside and connecting with friends and families.

In the strict traditional ceremonies, held in a tipi around a blazing fire, there are four distinct roles: the *Roadman,* who conducts the ceremony, guiding the participants along the "good, red road"; the *Fireman,* who tends the fire in the middle and also monitors who leaves to go out to relieve themselves – which is only permitted when someone is not singing; the *Cedarman,* who provides cedar branches for cleansing; and the *Drummer,* who provides the rhythm back-up with a water-filled drum to whoever is singing. A special role is reserved for the *Water Woman,* who provides fresh water for each participant when they exit from the tipi at dawn after an all-night ceremony.

In the traditional ceremonies one peyote chant after another is sung, the singer usually accompanying himself with a rattle and accompanied by the drummer. The chants may be traditional songs – often not with words, just with rhythmic syllables, handed down from one *peyotero* to another. In more loosely adapted ceremonies, participants may "channel" their own inspired songs, and "anglos" may be permitted to sing English-language or mixed syllabic chants. The main constant is the fast, insistent rhythm provided by the drummer.

The Peyote Way Church of God

In the late 1960s, having migrated from the East Coast, I came into contact with Immanuel Pardeahtan Trujillo, usually known as *Mana*, who was the son of a French mother and Apache father, a painter and potter, US Army veteran, who had for many years functioned as a *Roadman* in the NAC. He had visited our project in Millbrook, NY, and was interested in exploring other psychedelic substances besides the traditional peyote. I met with him in Colorado where he was living at the time and we discussed creating a new hybrid ritual form. He had become disenchanted with the rigidity of the NAC, when the traditionalists would not allow the two children he had with a white woman to be eligible to participate, since their genetic heritage was less than 50% Indian.

Mana and I arranged for an outdoor group session for a small group of his friends, using LSD as the catalyst and agreeing on the following simple and safe format: we started out sitting around a fire, sharing our intentions and partaking of the medicine. Then people went off in different directions to pursue their own individual visions, but the agreement was that you would remain visible to the one person, in rotation, who remained by the fire. People who wanted to talk and share experiences would come to the fire and those who wanted to commune alone with their spirits would stay in their further-out orbit.

In 1977 the *Peyote Way Church of God* was founded on a 160-acre ranch in an isolated area of Southern Arizona near Mount Graham, the traditional sacred mountain of the Apaches, by Immanuel Trujillo, Anne Zapf and Matthew Kent. This Church adopted many of the dietary doctrines of Mormonism – i.e. no alcohol, tobacco, caffeine, white sugar or white flour and very limited consumption of meat; but regard the stewarding, growing, ingesting and distributing of the "Holy Sacrament Peyote" as core religious belief and practice. Apart from that, the Church advocates a holistic life style, the pursuit of personal experience of the Holy Spirit within, self-discipline, compassion, non-violence, selfless service, recognition of the central role of the female as the giver of life and a family-oriented cottage industry.

They have fought thirty years of legal battles in the courts of Arizona to protect and preserve their religious use of peyote. They do not conduct group peyote ceremonies like the NAC – instead their practice is a solitary *Spirit Walk*, akin to what some other Native American traditions call a Vision Quest. After a 24-hour fast, the individual is guided and supported to go out into the desert mountain wilderness alone, with a supply of the peyote buttons, camping overnight, to pray and fast and to seek visions.

Traditional mushroom ceremonies of the Mazatec Indians

The traditional mushroom ceremonies of the Mazatec, and other tribes in Mexico, were brought to the attention of the Western world in the late 1950s through the writings of R. Gordon Wasson, who described his encounter with the *curandera* Maria Sabina in an article with photographs in LIFE magazine in 1957. With this article the survival of a pre-Conquest sacred mushroom ceremony exploded into Western consciousness. The vision-inducing mushrooms were (and are) revered by the Indians for providing deep spiritual insight and healing.

After Wasson and Albert Hofmann had identified *psilocybin* as the psychoactive ingredient in the mushrooms, this became the substance that was used in the early Harvard studies initiated by Leary and his associates. At present, the use of synthetic psilocybin is continuing to be tested in controlled double-blind experiments for the treatment of addictions, obsessions and anxiety. Meanwhile, thanks to the efforts of the McKenna brothers and others, methods of home cultivation of the mushrooms were developed and support a vast international underground network of mushroom growers.

In my book *Sacred Mushrooms of Visions – Teonanácatl* I describe some of the variations that the rituals of this ancient sacred medicine have undergone in modern times. The basic features adopted and preserved from the Mazatec traditional ceremonies are: *one*, a group of people sit in a circle in a darkened room, which is lit only by a candle until the mushrooms are handed out and then is totally darkened; *two*, the healer-leader sings and chants, invoking the spirits and calling them to help heal the presenting patient. Maria Sabina's songs and chants, which have been recorded, could go on for hours – blending prayer-words with word-less syllables and exclamations. In contemporary ceremonies the healer-singer may be accompanied by a drum or rattle; some also play guitar and accompany themselves singing.

The mushrooms, even compared to other visionary substances, seem to particularly favor the speech and song centers of the brain, as well as the humor centers if they exist – since some sessions are punctuated by much giggling and laughing. After all, the Mazatecs referred to these mushrooms as *los niños*, "the little children," elfin-like spirits that seem to like to amuse the celebrants. In contemporary culture the mushroom ceremonies may involve much laughter – although traditional healers would not countenance any distraction from the serious intent of the ceremonies. I have also witnessed celebrants use the mushrooms in outdoor ceremonies in nature – here the brilliant colored networks of light may be superimposed on the trees, rocks, fields and flowers of the surrounding nature.

Amazonian mestizo ayahuasca ceremonies

The traditional shamanic ceremony involving *ayahuasca* or *yagé* is a loosely structured experience, in which a small group of people come together with a respectful, spiritual attitude to share a profound inner journey of healing and transformation. In the Amazonian rainforest towns and villages there are *mestizo* practitioners who offer ayahuasca ceremonies in their local communities, as well as to Western tourists seeking possible healing insights or breakthroughs. A monetary contribution for the ceremony is usually expected – and most Westerners are happy to make a contribution to a Third World village economy.

The degree of experience and training of the guide will vary considerably. Anthropologists such as Luis Eduardo Luna have documented how the initiations and trainings of a traditional *ayahuasquero* can involve many months and even years of practice, with special diets and prolonged fasting. The purpose of the preliminary fasting is to purify the body of toxins so that the eliminative action of the ayahuasca medicine is not so intense and harsh. Some of the most violent and painful vomiting reactions I have seen in ayahuasca sessions occurred with long-term habitual smokers. On the other hand, I have seen experienced ayahuasca users, including a six-months pregnant woman, vomit easily in a relaxed and painless manner, in the early part of a session.

Ayahuasca ceremonies are typically conducted for about a dozen or so participants, who may sit and/or lie arranged around the floor of a simple house with windows open to the night air. Sessions conducted at night-time, like the eye-shades in medical sessions, function to focus the attention of the voyager on inner visions, not the outer scenery. The *ayahuasquero* may say some initial prayers and then passes out the brew. During the ceremony he or she sings the *icaros,* the healing songs that function to invoke the spirits which that particular healer has connected with, during his or her apprenticeship.

In marked and obvious contrast to the Western model of medicine, here both the doctor and the patient take the medicine and the healer sings songs, which invoke the spirits, who do the healing on the patient. There is no interpretation or analysis of the visions by the guide – nor even interest in hearing about them. Westerners who attend such ceremonies will need to do their own interpretation and analysis of visions and guidance received, according to the intentions they have brought to the sessions.

The preparation in these *mestizo* ayahuasca ceremonies is minimal. Of course, in the healer's local community he or she may know the participants personally and is likely familiar with their issues and families – they are neighbors and friends. For Western tourist visitors, the ceremonial leader may not even speak English. He usually does not have any access to their history, nor is knowledge of the personal history considered relevant. There is no history taking or declaring of intentions, nor is there any follow-up afterwards. Everything is done by the "spirits," who know what to do. For

Westerners used to a medical model or even a group psychotherapy model – there is none of that. Of course the individual participants can and do provide their own intentional preparation and integration. This is the main contrast of the Amazonian mestizo paradigm with the hybrid shamanic psychotherapeutic models to be discussed below which typically involve extensive preparation and integration.

Brazilian religious ceremonies with ayahuasca (UDV)

In addition to the indigenous and mestizo curing ceremonies there are three new folk religions in Brasil that incorporate the use of ayahuasca – the *Santo Daime, União do Vegetal (UDV)* and *Barquinia.* Two of these syncretic religious movements were founded by rubber tappers in the early part of the 20th century and all three have spread through the urban centers in Brazil, building dozens of churches with tens of thousands of adherents. In the last thirty years or so these religions have also gained followers and built churches in North America, Europe, Australia and Japan. Although the details of the ceremonies vary, for all of them the drinking of ayahuasca tea, also called *daime* or *hoasca,* is the central element of their religious practice. They are recognized as *bona fide* religious organizations in Brazil, where their use of ayahuasca tea is legal. In the US, Europe and elsewhere, they are semi-underground, being subject to occasional arrests and prosecution of church leaders and members, if local authorities learn of them.

If we define shamanism as an ecstatic journey by a shaman into alternate realms of reality for healing or divination, then the ayahuasca churches don't practice pure forms of shamanism. The intention of these churches, like mainstream Christian churches or

Jewish synagogues, is to practice and foster devotion to a ethical-religious life and communal belief system and to contribute to social improvement. They are not focused on nor particularly interested in the individuals having healings or transpersonal spiritual experiences. I remember one time in Brazil where I attended one of the ceremonies of the UDV, I asked one of the participants about the experience they had with the medicine in the ceremony. He didn't understand the question – which was as strange to him as it would be to a member of a Christian congregation coming out of Sunday church services!

Santo Daime is a highly syncretic tradition, combining Christian and non-denominational spiritual and indigenous elements. It was founded in the 1920s by a Afro-Brazilian rubber tapper named Raimundo Irineu Serra, who had been initiated into the use of ayahuasca by Peruvian Indian shamans. He was given a vision of a Woman on the Moon, who described herself as the "Queen of the Forest" and instructed him to establish a church, in which the drinking of the ayahuasca tea was to be the central ceremony. After Master Irineu died in 1971, leadership of the new church fell to Padrinho Sebastiao, another rubber tapper, with highly developed mediumistic abilities, who further organized the religious community. At first located in the outskirts of Rio Branco in the Upper Amazon, it subsequently established a community deeper in the Amazon rainforest near Mapiá, where 400 people now live on their land devoted whole-heartedly to the practice of a sustainable life-style and the spiritual practices of *Santo Daime*. Members and leaders of the Church travel regularly in Europe and the United States, where they have several centers with thriving communities.

The ayahuasca tea :

The tea is referred to as /*Daime*/ (which translates as "Give me," i.e. it is a request for divine blessing). There are no written texts giving teachings or doctrines. There are no sermons. There are hymn books, containing dozens of simple devotional songs, praising divine forces in cosmos and nature and exhortations to a good life. The words and melodies of these hymns are said to have been channeled by the founders and elders of the church. These songs are sung by the people participating in the ceremonies. The celebrants, after drinking the *Daime* tea, are singing the songs while also dancing in simple four step movements to the left and the right. Three or four musicians with guitars and rattles accompany the communal singing and dancing, and the positioning and alignment of the dancers is closely monitored and guided. Men and women participants in the ceremonies are arranged in lines on opposite sides of the room, dressed in white and dark blue. An inward concentration is recommended as is the maintenance of the structure. If people feel ill or faint, they are supported and may leave the room until they can return.

I have participated in *Santo Daime* ceremonies several times and met many of the members of the church, both Brazilian and North American. Here too, generating communal ecstasies and feelings of connectedness with all life, seems to be more important than pursuing individual visions. However, there are also other ceremonies where the participants just sit in quiet meditation, without music. The *Santo Daime* ceremonies reminded me of old-time gospel prayer meetings, with their exuberant singing, hand-clapping and stomping/swaying.

The /*União Do Vegetal (UDV)*/ was also founded by a rubber trapper, José Gabriel da Costa, in 1961. The UDV describes itself as a "Christian Spiritist" religion that uses the *hoasca* tea as a form of communion in their church services. They have several hundred adherents in various countries. Their ceremonies have a very different feel. If the *Santo Daime* are like gospel sessions, the *UDV* are like Puritan/Protestant church meetings. Participants sit on straight-back chairs in rows in a day-lit room, with a bright light-bulb in the ceiling and listen to sermons delivered by senior members of the clergy, who are sitting around a long table in the center. Nothing in the set-up is conducive to going within and seeking visions. Some of the *maestres* sitting at the table will sing songs, give sermons and sometimes answer questions, but everyone else just sits and prays quietly. I attended several of the ceremonies and did not resonate with them at all – they reminded me of a cross between a Protestant church service and an AA meeting. As I mentioned, there seemed to be no interest whatsoever in the visions people might be having. However, that is just my personal inclination, and I respect the good social work the *UDV* has done in their communities, countering alcoholism and drug abuse and encouraging responsibility for family and children.

The third of the Brazilian churches, *Barquinia* (derived from the image of a barque as a vessel, like the Buddhist idea of a vessel to cross the ocean of illusion) is much smaller in numbers than the other two and I have personally only attended one or two gatherings. It is more connected to the Brazilian spiritist religion *Umbanda*, which involves cultivating mediumistic connections to ancestral spirit guides and teachers and the Afro-Brazilian deities known as *orixas*. In these churches, there is an altar in the center of the room, along with a group of musicians who play vigorous rhythmic music. After taking the ayahuasca, celebrants dance around the perimeter of the central altar, invoking the *orixas* and singing songs of healing and celebration. Unlike the *UDV* and

Santo Daime churches, both of which have numerous branch centers in North America and Europe, the *Barquinia* is little known outside of Brazil.

Elements of hybrid entheogenic ceremonies

In the past 30 years or so I have been a participant–observer in a large number of circle rituals, in both Europe and North and South America, involving hundreds of individuals, many of them repeatedly, in ongoing ceremonial practices. The entheogenic substances involved in these circles have included psilocybe mushrooms, ayahuasca, San Pedro cactus preparations, iboga, LSD, mescaline, MDMA, 2CB and others. My interest has been focused on the nature of the psychospiritual transformations undergone by participants in these circles. I will focus on those circles that have as their main focus and intention psychospiritual healing and growth as well as visionary experience. I will not include in my discussion those group ceremonies, like "raves" or similar events, which may involve some degree of psychospiritual intention, but where the primary purpose is recreational.

As I indicated, in the traditional indigenous and mestizo rituals with mushrooms and ayahuasca, as well as in the Brazilian churches, there is no declaration of intentions or much by way of preparation. Yet this is usually a most important aspect and distinguishing feature of contemporary practice, along with the cultivation of a respectful, spiritual attitude. Experienced entheogenic explorers understand the importance of "set" and therefore devote considerable attention to clarifying their intentions with respect to healing and divination. They also understand the importance of "setting" and therefore devote considerable care to arranging a peaceful place and time, filled with natural beauty and free from outside distractions or interruptions.

An approximate guideline many have found useful is the following: *devote equal amounts of time to preparation beforehand and integration afterwards, as the duration of the ceremony itself.* Thus, for a typical four hour entheogen experience, such groups would spend about four hours in preparation and four hours in integration. If the ceremony is held indoors, as most are, there may be candles along with other objects on the altar, but there is generally a preference for low light, or semi-darkness, and/or the use of eye shades to facilitate an inward focus of attention.

In these hybrid therapeutic-shamanic circle rituals, although there is wide variation in the complexity and details of structure, most of the following elements from traditional indigenous circles are preserved to some degree. We will discuss each of them in turn: 1) the structure of a circle, with participants either sitting or lying; 2) the invocation of spirits; 3. clarifying intentions for healing and/or vision; 4. ceremonial altar, amulets and talismans; 5. the role of prayer, mantra and mudra; 6. chanting, singing and music; 7. the council format and talking stick practice; 8. the role of the elder, leader or guide; 9. egalitarian groups with rotating leadership.

The presence of an experienced elder or guide, sometimes with one or more assistants, who conducts the ceremony and monitors the flow of experience and the safety of the participants is by far the most commonly found format. In most situations the specific ritual elements are implicitly accepted as part of the structure offered by the guide. In self-organizing groups with rotating conductors, these elements are then also ideally subject to prior agreements, to avoid distracting and conflicting discussions about such issues as the choice of music.

1. The circle structure. The format of a group of humans meeting together in a circle is one of the most ancient and universal forms of human communication and fellowship. The Arthurian Knights of the Round Table used this form to symbolize their break from the hierarchical structures of church and kingship. Native Americans use it for all their political councils as well. Whether meeting in political council or spiritual ceremony, in a circle everyone can see and hear everyone equally. When there are specific temporary leadership or guiding roles, as in the Native American Church peyote ceremonies, everyone is still basically in the circle. People may be sitting on the floor or on chairs, but no one is sitting on a throne and there is no priest with their back turned to the congregation.

Participants may sit or lie arranged in the circle, or alternate between sitting and lying. If lying down, it is generally recommended that participants lie with their head toward the center, and their feet outward; if sitting, with their feet tucked under. The reason for this is that according to yoga teachings, the discharge of toxic energy residues is downward and outward through the legs and feet, as the purifying energies flow down from the light-centers above the head. In India, when people gather to hear a discourse from a spiritual teacher, they always sit in the cross-legged position, as does the guru, so such toxic elements are discharged and neutralized down into the earth. If there is an altar with sacred objects, candles and flowers in the center, the toxic discharges are directed outward, while people are, psychically and energetically, "putting their heads together" in the center.

In entheogenic group ceremonies, according to preference, some participants may sit in cross-legged position (again, with feet tucked under), with a supportive back-rest. In some ceremonies participants may alternate between the lying position pursuing their inner visions with eyes closed or covered; and sitting in circle, focused on the fire or the altar in the middle. Participants may then take turns singing, with or without a drum or a rattle, or speaking, perhaps with a speaking staff or object. As ayahuasca ceremonies have spread to the West and the North, most people have found it expedient to adopt a seated position as is customary in the South American ayahuasca sessions, often in a large bean-bag or other easy chair. This is for the very practical reason that sudden vomiting episodes can occur without warning, which can create house-keeping and body-management issues if the person has to first pull themselves up from a lying position.

In many or most groups of travelers, married couples will usually sit and/or lie next to each other in the circle and this feels natural enough. However, in some of the long-term groups of seasoned travelers which I have observed, married couples may wisely decide not to lie next to each other. The subtle energy-fields of such couples tend to be intertwined and entangled with one another – which may confuse the perception and interpretations of things seen and felt. A ceremony participant may be unable to sort out whether the images and thought-emotion patters that are being entheogenically perceived are one's own or the partner's. The spatial separation makes it easier to practice that temporary disentanglement – which will be followed at the end of course by renewed interconnection.

2. The invocations of spirits. The chanting or speaking of prayer-like invocations at the beginning of a ceremony with entheogenic substances is near-universal among the indigenous users of these substances, as well as in the ayahuasca churches. It is absent in the sessions based on the clinical and scientific paradigm – though participants may silently speak their own private prayers. According to my observations over the past 30 years in what I am calling hybrid entheogenic group ceremonies, prayer-like invocations are rarely offered, except by those individuals who have adopted a ritual from their own indigenous ceremonial teachers, or by those associated with one or another of the neo-pagan churches active in North America and Europe. This may be due to lingering discomfort in many Western people with explicit expression of religious or spiritual concepts or beliefs. The secret question or reservation some people seem to hold is: "but I don't really believe in spirits – or do I?" For myself, having grown up within the normal 20th century agnostic, materialist worldview, for whom experiencing a drug-induced state was at first considered a scientific experiment, the acceptance of the possible reality status of spirits took quite a long time.

There were several key converging points of influence in the evolution of my expanded worldview. One was my participation in the *Agni Yoga* (also called *Actualism*) meditation training, in which clairvoyant perception of spirit beings and subtle non-material energy-fields evolved naturally though intermittently as a consequence of the practice. Another influence was the experience I had with wilderness vision quests, facilitated by Stephen Foster and Meredith Little of the *School of Lost Borders*, in the Mojave Desert of Southern California. I was impressed and delighted at the simple down-to-earth way that Stephen and Meredith would speak the "calling-in" of the spirits of the desert and the plants and animals, while sitting on the ground, holding a feather and rattle, and distributing smoke from a shell with burning sage. There was no trace of artifice or assumed holiness. They seemed to take it for granted that you could speak with nature spirits as easily as you could speak with your relatives on the phone. You just call the number – and the "number" to call is the *name* of the spirit-being you are invoking. In these wilderness vision quests, there was no ingestion of any substances, in fact we were fasting – so one would not be distracted by any wondering over whether we were perceiving a so-called "drug effect."

A third line of influence for me was my connection with and learning from the anthropologist and educator Michael Harner, who has staked his academic reputation on the explicit affirmation of the experiential reality of spirits – beings that one can connect with in dreams or waking state visions or shamanic journeys – without having the impulse or need to categorize them as "hallucinations" or "illusions" or even "symbols." Harner's and Foster's approach to visions of spirits exemplify the "radical empiricism" of William James or the "first-person empiricism" of the Dalai Lama. It is in that spirit that I've developed over the years a practice of explicitly invoking spirits at the beginning of every entheogenic individual session or group gathering.

I have published some of these invocation prayer-poems, and give the texts in the *Epilogue*. I wish to emphasize that I do not recommend that one read the invocation prayers from this or any other written text – unless it is by way of personal preparation for one's own individual journey. In groups, it is far better if the person leading or guiding the session speaks the invocation of spirits with whom they have personally established a connection, and omit invoking any spirits with whom they have not personally connected in their own experience. It would be like talking about someone as if you'd personally become acquainted with them and made friends with them – when actually you had only heard about them. The often heard question "do you believe in spirits?" is as irrelevant as "do you believe in people." More to the point is that you invoke and communicate with the beings and persons you've met and are open to meeting others. Then you do not let yourself be distracted or blocked by self-critical judgments about whether you're just "making it up."

In my book *Alchemical Divination* (p. 41-58) I give a detailed description of seven phases of divination rituals, which I will draw on here. To repeat, it is more important that one invoke those spirits with which one already made a connection or has an ongoing relationship than connecting with "all spirits." The latter formula could in fact hold a certain danger, since you cannot assume all spirits are necessarily well-disposed toward you – anymore than you could make that assumption regarding all people or animals that you meet.

The first set of spirits to invoke and connect with are the *spirits of four directions*, the *spirits of the place* and the *spirits of the time*. The spirits of the four directions are planetary spirits – perhaps even extending their reach beyond planet Earth through the solar system and the galaxy beyond. Calling upon the spirits of the four directions, starting with the East and followed by South, West and North (going *sunwise*, as our pagan friends call it), is a way of localizing ourselves and becoming conscious of the particular place where we are on Earth. Indigenous cultures and pagan traditions around the world always begin their ceremonies and meetings with prayers to the spirits of the four directions. Naturally, the prayers spoken in different traditions and locales will associate different symbolic elements, animals, colors and qualities to the directions.

Aligning with and honoring the spirits of the particular place. In ancient Roman culture, each place had its own protective spirit, the *genius loci*. The particular forms and forces of the ecosystem, the landforms and waterways of a place, the plants, animals and humans that live in that place give it a unique character that we want to honor and respect.

Harmonizing with the spirits of the planetary cycles of time. Just as particular places are associated with particular spirits or deities, so are the cycles of time. It makes a difference what phase of the day we do our meditation divination: traditionally, evening twilight affords an opening between the worlds, and nighttime in general is considered better for clairvoyant "seeing" compared to daytime. As our part of the Earth turns away from the Sun, awareness expands into the cosmos and we see the stars we cannot see when we are blinded by daytime sunlight. The phase of the lunar cycle we're in and the seasonal cycle of the year, with the four great cosmic gateways of solstice and equinox, also profoundly affect the quality and efficacy of our meditations, dreams and divinations.

In the *Epilogue* I offer two versions of a four-directions prayer, as well as general invocations of the spirits of place and time, that one can and should adapt to local and particular circumstances and conditions. In contrast to the spirits of animals and spirit guides, our relationship with the spirits of the four directions, of place and time, are not personal: we do not seek their aid and counsel for our projects, rather we align and harmonize with them in order to humbly adapt to the circumstances in which we find ourselves.

Invoking spirit allies from the animal world. Variously called "power animals," "spirit animals," or "totemic animals" (when associated with a whole clan), animal spirits have been the allies, guides and teachers of shamanic practicioners since the most ancient hunter-gatherer and Stone Age times. We are speaking here of invoking, not so much a particular animal that we love, such as a pet dog or cat (although they could be included in the invocation), but rather the spirit or deity of a wild animal species – of *Buffalo* or *Wolf*, not this or that particular buffalo or wolf. The word "wild" is related to the word "will" – the wild creature is the "self-willed"

36

and sovereign, not subject to domestication or the will of another. In cultivating our connection and friendship with animal spirits we are reminded of our own wild and indigenous evolutionary heritage on planet Earth.

ANIMALS

Animals, as Arthur Young has said, are Nature's great experiments in movement – and so we find that the animal allies can help us when we need to learn to move, whether physically with more flexibility, or emotionally and mentally out of fixed positions and patterns. I recommend that in the course of shamanic and alchemical practice, one seek to develop a relationship with an ally from each of the main classes of animals, the mammals of land and sea, the reptiles, amphibians, birds and insects – each are specialist teachers of evolutionary strategy and ecological adaptation.

Invoking plant and fungal helper spirits. Whereas animals are humankind's most direct evolutionary ancestors and relatives, plants and fungi are the two other kingdoms of multi-cellular life on this planet. Great webs of symbiotic interdependence and mutuality link the animal, plant and fungal realms. Animals breathe in the oxygen the plants exhale and plants absorb the carbon dioxide the animals exhale in the great atmospheric dance – a complex set of relationships that humans are now catastrophically disrupting. Plants grow and produce the food that nourishes the animals; mammals, birds and insects eat and transport the packages of seeds and pollen, enabling plants to propagate; fungi decompose and recycle dead plant and animal matter, nourishing the roots of trees through their vast, subterranean mycelial nets.

In connecting with spirits of plant and fungal life, we honor the nourishment, the medicines and the inspiration of beauty we receive from these realms. For shamanic and alchemical practitioners the spirits of the mind-assisting, perception-amplifying, entheogenic plants and fungi are of particular interest. The spirits of those plants or fungi or medicine substances that are involved as consciousness-expanding media in the ceremony should be specifically acknowledged. It's like we're embarking on a journey, accompanied by a friend we've journeyed with before, and we naturally recall our friendship and collaboration. From plant and fungal spirits we can learn many lessons, but particularly the lessons of growth and interconnection, of extending and nourishing our relationships with humans and more-than-human beings and life-forms in the multiple worlds of life on planet Earth.

Invoking spirits of the mineral and elemental realms. Science recognizes carbon-based life-forms at the level of protists and microbes but draws the distinction to non-life at the mineral realm. Indigenous shamanic traditions and their mythologies, as well as hermetic and esoteric teachings recognize living spirit intelligence in the inorganic realms as well. This is the realm that affords the material substrate and foundation for evolving life, and for the human constructed environment. Mineral elements provide sources of food and medicines to humans, crystals in microscopes and telescopes amplify perception of normally invisible realms of nature, precious stones inspire our visual sense of beauty. Metallic minerals are the prime sources of our technologies and the instruments of knowledge and science, of art and culture, and of destruction and warfare. Precious stones and metals provide a store of wealth and currency medium in virtually all modern societies.

In the shamanic and alchemical traditions the spirits of stone and earth, called *gnomes* or *dwarves* in Nordic mythology, are not regarded as compassionate guides or personal "familiars" the way animal and plant spirits can be. However, the spirits of earth-stone, as well as of the other elements of water, air and fire, are recognized and respected for their autonomy and power, and one can tune in with them and learn from them. The old alchemists called their body of knowledge the "philosophers' stone," or also the "water-stone of the wise." We can and should learn to be more conscious and considerate of the deep and complex interconnections we as humans have with this realm – especially as we are letting our obsessions with the technologies of weaponry, war and wealth destroy the foundations of civilization.

Invoking the spirits of our ancestors and human relations, as well as elders, spirit guides and deities. Maintaining and cultivating the connections with the spirits of deceased ancestors is probably the single most significant feature that distinguishes the shamanic indigenous worldview from the modern. I have sat in many native ceremonies and listened to the elders invoke the spirits of their ancestors, asking for their blessings, as naturally and obviously as we would ask for our elders' blessings when still alive.

In my psychotherapy practice I have come to appreciate that connecting and reconciling with deceased ancestors and family members, as in multi-generational family systems therapy, can have a hugely healing impact. As we care for our children and grandchildren and want the best for them and wish to guide them in their life-ways, so our ancestors are those who know us very well, care for us and represent our best supporting back-up team in dealing with life's challenges. But our ancestral spirits cannot connect to us if we are not receptive, or have derogatory and judgmental attitudes towards them, and even less if we believe they don't exist anymore because they are "dead." So we can invoke them with simple, basic gratitude and respect for the thread of life we have received from them – without having to judge whether they were "good" or "bad" people.

Connecting with our genetic ancestors naturally leads us to also invoke all our other *human relations.* The relatives of family, clan and ethnicity are those with whom our lives are interwoven by virtue of birth. The relations established in our formative years may often be the focus of our divination inquiries, as we seek to heal dysfunctional patterns forged in the crucible of family life. In addition, there are the human relations of "elective affinity," of romantic, erotic love and partnership, of friendship and collegiality, of cooperation and community. Each one of us lives in an open-ended web of human relations, of mutuality and exchange. The boundary of our network of human relations is given by the name: although we can and should encounter all human beings with egalitarian respect, *our relatives are those we know by name* and who call us by name, and with whom our lives are interwoven in multiple ways.

Similarly, we invoke with gratitude the blessings of our *spiritual ancestors and human elders,* mentors, teachers and guides, whose life-wisdom has inspired and continue to inspire us. Some of these spiritual ancestors and teachers may be known to thousands or millions – Buddhists would invoke Gautama Buddha and their Buddhist teachers and gurus, Christians call upon Jesus of Nazareth, Mother Mary and whatever saints and wise ones they're connected with. Others of our human elders and mentors may be known to only a few – what counts is the spiritual connection we as individuals have with them. We may also invoke human-like spirit guides that we've connected with, that we know only through inner meditative experience, and not in the time-space world of historical reality.

Also in this phase of preparation for the divination we call upon the *deities and divinities* with whom we have or wish to have a guiding, counseling, inspiring relationship. In the polytheistic animistic worldview of indigenous peoples, and of our own ancestors in ancient times, the beings called "gods" and "goddesses" are regarded as really existing in the same way that deceased human ancestors really exist – in a different, but not separate world. Many individuals in our time have come to develop and cultivate a spiritual relationship with one or another of the deities known in European, Asian, African or Native American mythology. For example, as part of the spiritual feminist renaissance in our time, many women (and men) have occupied themselves with images of the Goddess, whether as *Isis* or *Shakti* or *Kwan Yi*n or any of Her countless forms, inspiring their artistic creative and spiritual practice. I myself have had, as I related in *The Well of Remembrance*, a teaching and counseling relationship with *Odin*, the knowledge-seeking Nordic god of shamans and poets.

The gods and goddesses can be thought of as the ancestors, spirit guides and teachers of a whole people, or culture, or religious community. Their appearance, in our visions and meditations and recorded in the religious mythic art of all cultures, is human-like though greater, and may at times, as in Egyptian and Old European imagery and mythology, have blended features of animals and humans. Like our deceased human ancestors, they exist in the higher-frequency dimensions beyond our human time-space world, where we may communicate with them in our dreams and divinations.

The multiple dimensions of planet Earth and the cosmos beyond are teeming with supra-dimensional spirit beings, gods and goddesses of inconceivable diversity, brilliance and power. How could it be otherwise, knowing what we now know about the vastness and diversity of stars and planets in the Universe? In our time, as our civilization is confronted by global challenges of unprecedented difficulty and urgency, the ancient legends of deities walking among and communicating with humans on Earth, have taken on a new life: thousands (perhaps millions) of individuals on all continents have reported sightings of space-ships (called UFOs), obviously not from our world, cruising peacefully through our skies. Thousands (perhaps millions) of others have reported contact and communication with alien beings (called ETs) from star-systems and planets beyond Earth. Some of these contacts have involved actual meetings and interactions in the time-space physical dimension, with others the contact and communication has been on the intermediate dimensions, in dreams, visions or meditative states of consciousness.

When, in the practice of divination, we encounter such god-like beings from other world, we should relate to them as we would to any other autonomous being, human or more-than-human, in the time-space world or beyond – with equanimity, respect and compassion. By remaining centered with light-fire awareness, we can most clearly enter into a communicative exchange that will be relevant to our intentions and questions, and avoid entanglement with beings, whether earthly or extra-terrestrial, that have a manipulative or exploitative agenda.

3. *Articulating and clarifying intentions or questions:* All divination practices involve a process of seeking answers to a question, or focusing an intention. It could be said intention is in many ways a key to the understanding of any state of consciousness. Studies of EEG recordings in awake subjects have shown that a particular wave-form in a specific brain region can be registered fractions of a second before a movement is made in response to a request or command. Any state of consciousness (whether "altered" or "ordinary")

can best be understood if one inquires into the set or intention, that preceded or accompanied the catalyst that triggered the transition of consciousness. Intention, or "interest" as William James phrased it, controls the selective function of attention, which in turn determines what it is we perceive. If our attention and therefore perception is not guided by our conscious intention or interest, then it may be captured, or captivated, by whatever attractive, intense, insistent or prominent stimulus patterns present themselves to our senses. The essential formula then is the following:

intention (interest/question/wish/will)→attention→awareness

Asking a question is the basic gesture of receptivity and thus also a way of selectively focusing our attention. Intention and question are two equivalent and alternative ways of guiding our attention and perception, in both ordinary and non-ordinary states of consciousness. There is a dynamic (*yang*) and receptive (*yin*) polarity here: *intending* is more focused, directional, searching; and *asking* is more open, receptive, gathering. We can formulate the starting point of a divination in either way. In a divination for healing I can say, "I want to (or intend to) heal this wound or this relationship" or I could ask, "How can I heal this wound or relationship?" In a divination for envisioning the future, I can say, "I want to create or build this project" or I can ask, "How can I create or build this project?"

These two ways of deploying attention as we enter into a divinatory state of consciousness, may also be compared to the two ancient modes of hunters and gatherers: intending is like the stalking and tracking of the hunter, whereas asking is like the searching and collecting of the gatherer. The *arrow of intention* is narrowly aimed at the target, whether it be a memory or a vision. The *basket of search and research* is wide-angled and open to perceive information, whether from the past or the future.

Technological metaphors we can use to compare the two modes of searching are the *telescope* and the *antenna*. Intentional focus is narrow, as with a telescope, and thereby magnifies and amplifies the perception of the target. On the other hand, with an antenna system, we are holding a question as we orient the 'receiving dish' (of attention) towards a wide range of situations, to maximize our chances of perceiving information relevant to our quest.

The clarification of one's intention is the master key to having safe and productive experiences in any realm or state of consciousness, including meditative or psychedelic states, as well as the "ordinary" state of everyday functional awareness. Therefore we can say that the internal preparation for any divinatory inquiry begins by clarifying one's intentions or questions, for oneself. It is not particularly important that the intentions/questions are shared with others – that varies with the kind and format of the session.

In the *Introduction* I mentioned the six most common intentions/questions in entheogenic journeys (excluding the purely recreational): supporting healing or psychotherapy; supporting the overcoming of addictions; preparing the dying for their final passage; understanding states and dimensions of consciousness; enhancement of creativity and increased openness to religious/ mystical experience.

It is usually best to focus on one issue or question at a time in any particular inquiry. Relevant additional questions can be asked during the individual divination process, during the integration phase or in a subsequent divination on the same topic. In entheogenic sessions, the seeker typically may hold a particular question or set of questions in mind, whether for healing, visioning or both. Answers may be received in the course of the journey, sometimes right at the beginning – or sometimes at the end, or even after the journey is completed, in a night-time dream. Having formulated a clear divinatory question can then serve as a reference point to help interpret or understand some otherwise obscure or meaningless parts of the experience.

One can usefully distinguish the *divination phase* and the *integration phase*. In the divination phase you note the answers received to the question you articulated and suspend further interpretation of that answer. In an individual therapy situation, the interpretation may be discussed or considered immediately. In a group divination ritual it's usually better to just note the vision/answer received and leave the interpretation and analysis until a later time, when the drug effect has worn off and the usual faculties of the mind have returned. In the integration phase, the therapist might ask, or the person may ask themselves, "what answer did I get in response to my question, and what are the implications of that answer for myself and my life-world?"

4. Ceremonial altar or table. Amulets and talismans. There are two variations of a ceremonial table or altar that contemporary entheogenic circles have come to use: the altar may be on the ground in the center of the circle, or the altar may be on a table nearby. Objects such as candles, special stones, crystals, feathers, or other meaningful items may be placed for the duration of the ceremony, along with either spoken or silent prayers. The basic principle of the table or altar is to provide a place for sacred power objects that the shaman and the participants bring to the ceremony and that they may also use in the ceremony, or hold in their hands. These objects act to focus the spiritual intention and attention of the individual participants and add spiritual power to the group ceremony.

In the ceremonies of the Andean cultures using the San Pedro cactus there is a table with a "dark" side and a "light" side. Various objects and icons may be placed to symbolize or invoke the protective and beneficent spirits on the one hand and the destructive and malevolent spirits on the other, with the intention of keeping the two in balance with recognition and respect. Such a recognition of the equal reality status of "dark spirits" or "dark energy", which is common in indigenous and Eastern cultures makes many Westerners uncomfortable – probably because of the long and complex history of the European Inquisition and its centuries-long persecution of so-called "witchcraft" and "sorcery." Contemporary Western seekers may prefer to work with such elements and symbols along Jungian lines, using objects or representations of what are called "shadow" aspects of the psyche.

For most contemporary entheogenic voyagers, a table or altar figuratively connects with their shamanic healing and guiding spirits. Such a table or altar therefore could include pictures of loved ones, ancestors, children, teachers, guides – always including those that are deceased as well as the living. Some people bring pictures or objects associated with those relatives that the voyager wants to invoke for special healing, protection or assistance. Some may choose to include images of spiritual teachers, healers and guides such as Jesus, Mary, Buddha, Kwan Yin, Isis and Osiris, Christian saints, enlightened ones, mythic deities and/or personal spirit guides.

Those who have experience and training in the shamanic practices using the shamanic drumming journey and have established a connection with one or another power (or spirit or totemic) animal, may place objects on the altar associated with that animal – such as bones, feathers, claws, pieces of fur, horn, ivory, teeth and others; others may bring objects derived from or incorporating pieces of plants – such as leaves, dried flowers, roots, seeds, stalks, twigs, bark and others; still others may bring objects from the mineral realm – such as stones, jewels, crystals and others. All such personally meaningful objects may be placed on the altar in their raw and unprocessed form – or they may be incorporated in pieces of body adornment such as bracelets, scarves, rings, armbands, headbands, pendants and the like.

Some practitioners prefer to keep their sacred power objects in a special bag or pouch, as most Native Americans do, and only unwrap and display them in ceremony, holding them while saying their prayers. Others may place objects on the ceremonial altar that they also wear in ordinary life. Some may place on the altar an object that is used in their everyday life – that they want to imbue with special shamanic power and meaning. In some ceremonies, the participants may just keep their chosen object on or near their person, or as a wearable object.

What shamanic practitioners call "power objects" and some native traditions call "totems" are also known in the Western traditions of Wicca, witchcraft and ceremonial magic as *amulets* and *talismans*. These can consist of objects of mineral, metal, animal or plant origin, and may be inscribed or carved or encased in pendants, necklaces, pouches or the like, to be worn on the person. The main difference between the two is that amulets are said to be protective – against bad spirits or influences from others or the environment – whereas talismans, which may also be referred to as *touch-stones*, simply strengthen the connection of the individual to the higher realms of Spirit.

Precious and semi-precious stones are often used, both alone and in combination, as amulets and talismans. The violet amethyst stone has a traditional protective effect against poisoning, infection and intoxication, whether physical or psychic. Precious stones such as diamonds, rubies, emeralds and sapphires, as well as the precious metals gold and silver each have histories of thousands of years concerning their value in healing ceremonies, and may be incorporated as talismans in various ways in shamanic and entheogenic ceremonies. Certain psychic or sensitive individuals can sense or see, moving, multi-hued energy currents associated with precious stones, crystals and metals. Such energy currents may become visible in the heightened states of awareness induced by entheogens, especially in predisposed individuals.

I remember an incident from my early explorations with psychoactive substances that dramatically showed me the value of an amulet or "touch-stone." It was one of my first experiments with smoking DMT. As I inhaled the psychoactive smoke I found myself in a swirling cloud-like mass with no conceivable sense of direction or bodily identity. I had a ring with an amethyst stone on my finger. Without intention or suggestion, as I felt the touch of my finger with this ring, my attention was captured by a kind of rope or thread, which immediately took me back to the ring on my hand and into my body, sitting on the ground. Needless to say, I was impressed by the power of that object to safely ground me back to earth.

A talisman-like use of a touched stone is the so-called *churinga* stone, used by some Australian aboriginal tribes. This is usually a flat, polished stone or piece of wood, that can fit into a hand. It may be engraved with totemic emblems and secret geographic codes, that enable desert-walkers to find their way around their tribal territories. Entheogenic explorers who also go on wilderness vision quests, have found it valuable to incorporate such amulets, touch-stones and talismans into their practice.

If the ceremonial altar is set up on the floor in the center of a circle of voyagers, there is usually some kind of decorative cloth and an object, like a candle or a crystal, in the center and in each of the four directions. Some groups then mark each of the four directions with an additional object (candle, crystal) of some kind. Objects representing each of the four elements may be placed around the altar: feathers for the air element, a candle for fire, small branches with leaves and/or fruit and flowers for the earth element, and a bowl with water. There may also be other figurines in the middle – such as religious icons according to the predilections of the ceremonialist and the participants.

There are special portable fire-places that produce a non-odorous, smoke-less flame for indoor placement on a table or flat place in the center (they are commercially produced for the barbecue market). Participants can then focus their meditative attention on the fire in the center analogously to the way in the traditional peyote ceremony one stares into the fire in the middle. The constant yet always changing light of a burning flame has been a favored object of spiritual concentration and symbolism in all kinds of ceremonies since the most ancient times.

In some group ceremonies there may be a fire-container next to a bowl of water in the middle. Participants can then practice gazing at the fire and the water side by side. In my book *The Expansion of Consciousness* (p. 18) I reproduce a 17th century alchemical engraving titled "The Union of Fire and Water," which can be thought of as a symbolic portrayal of this process, also called *coniunctio*. It shows two figures with human-like heads, but flowing streams of energy instead of human bodies, sitting face to face, with further streams of energy connecting the tops of their heads together. I interpret this image as a representation of the yogic process of unifying the yang/male/fiery and yin/female/fluid energies within the body. So, in gazing at the physical fire and water in the middle of the circle one can consciously and intentionally link the inner processes of the alchemical *coniunctio* with the outer perception of fire and water side by side.

In some entheogenic ceremonies, the setting up of an altar in the middle is connected with the declaration of intentions. Participants take turns in placing their object on the altar cloth in the middle and declare their intentions for healing and visioning, as well as prayers they are invoking for their relatives or their communities. They may say something about what the object they are placing on the altar symbolizes to them and invoke their specific deities or spirit guides. I should mention however, that according to Michael Harner's observations in world-wide shamanic cultures, the identity of a particular shaman's power animals or spirit guide is best kept secret from strangers, as knowing it can give a potential enemy sorcerer or shaman a psychic advantage or a tool for causing harm. So depending on the context, prayers and invocations may be spoken aloud or murmured quietly to oneself.

5. *The role of prayer, mantra and mudra.* The use of mantras and prayers, whether spoken aloud or silently to oneself, are among key elements that distinguish intentional entheogenic practice from recreational use of psychedelic drugs. Some entheogenic circles have adopted a particular prayer, whether Buddhist, Christian, Jewish or Pagan as part of the invocation at the start of the ceremony. In pagan-inspired ceremonies and shamanic drumming journey circles the initial prayer may involve the invocation of particular

deities or guiding spirits, with whom the traveler has established a relationship. Some groups may use the Christian *Lord's Prayer*, or other poetic expression of a prayerful attitude, as for example from the wonderful collection *Earth Prayers From Around the World* (edited by Elizabeth Roberts and Elias Amidon).

The literal meaning of the word *mantra* is a kind of instrument, both for invoking ("calling in") the connection to a specific deity as well as cultivating a particular attitude, such as humility or reverence. It is asserted and believed that with such core mantras, both the semantic meaning and the actual sonic vibration of the mantra have spiritual significance. Some of the best-known mantric invocations that may be used in entheogenic as well as other spiritual ceremonies are: *O Great Spirit, Ave Maria, Om Mani Padma Hum, Om Nama Shivaya, Kyrié Eléison, Tat Tvam Asi, La Ilaha Illa'llah.* Furthermore, the history of thousands, maybe millions or hundreds of millions of devotees having repeated these mantras over the centuries, and repeating them now has added immense cumulative spiritual power to them.

In *Worlds Within and Worlds Beyond*, I described the practice, said silently to oneself, of what we, in our circle groups, have come to call the *Moses Mantra*.

> As related in the Bible, when Moses has the vision of an Angel of the Lord in a burning bush, and is given guidance to lead his people out of slavery into liberation, he is overcome with insecurity, and asks, "When I come unto the children of Israel, and shall say to them the God of your fathers has sent me to you; and they shall say to me, what is his name? What shall I say to them? And God said to Moses, I AM THAT I AM: Thus shalt thou say unto the children of Israel." (*Exodus 3*)

This mantra is an *affirmation of essence being*, not calling upon any external authority or assertion of belief or particular doctrine or quality of our person – but simply standing firm in our essential beingness (*op.cit.* p.40).

In the Indian yoga of sound practice (*shabda yoga*), there are also singular "seed" syllables, known as *bija-mantras*, open vowel sounds which can be spoken as part of a mantra or intoned as part of a long drawn-out chant. They do not have linguistic "meaning" in the usual sense, but are thought to activate particular chakras. The best-known example is the *bija-mantra OM* or *AUM*, which may be part of a prayer phrase, as shown above, or sounded as a long-drawn out tone. *OM* or *AUM* is said to express and energize the oneness of the individual with the divine and the cosmic. Other seed-mantras are *RAM, HUM, VAM, TRAM, HRIH.*

The theory and practice of mantra chanting, toning, the relationship to sound frequencies and the connections between vibrations and dimensions of consciousness are vast and far beyond the scope of this book, with its focus on practices connected with medicine circles. The interested reader is referred to the excellent teachings and writings on these topics by Silvia Nakkach, Don Campbell and Jonathan Goldman. In the circles I have been involved with, we have made it a practice to intone some of the best-known mantras, not only as an initial invocation, but also during the session, after a time of inner exploration, to sit and chant these mantras together. This has the effect of adding a centered attitude to the visions one has seen and still is seeing, a kind of mantra-empowered mindfulness with holistic right-brain focus, without diverting attention to the details of left-brained verbal descriptions.

Hand positions, known in the Indian tantric practice as *mudras*, may also be added to the mantra chanting, or practiced silently while sitting in circle. Holding a *mudra* while intoning a *mantra* adds to the power of both practices. Probably the best known of these hand positions is the *Buddha mudra* - sitting cross-legged, with the left hand holding the right-hand at the abdomen, thumbs touching, so the whole body is contained within a circle. These *mudras* are familiar to us from thousands of images, in paintings and sculptures – with many viewers perhaps not realizing they also portray a practice. Another *mudra* frequently seen in Buddhist art is performed by holding the left hand in the lap and holding the right hand palm forward, fingers pointing upward: this *mudra* signifies "Fear Not," because the open empty hand holds no weapon and hence represents a greeting-contact between equals without threat or domination.

6. *Chanting, singing and music.* In the shamanic and ceremonial practices of the peoples of the Northern hemisphere in Europe, Asia and America, where psychogenic plants or substances are rarely used, it is primarily the rhythmic beat of the drum that drives the shamanic voyager though non-ordinary, visionary states – and returns him or her to ordinary reality after the healing or vision mission has been accomplished. It was said that "the beat of the drum is the beat of the hooves of the shaman's power animal." This is the spiritual technology of the drumming journey, which has been re-introduced into the modern world of shamanic practitioners through the work of anthropologist Michael Harner and his associates. The drumming here does not consist of complex rhythmic patterns as these are used in various forms of music. Rather it is a form of "auditory driving" in which the simple beat of the drum at frequencies in the alpha range (8-10 cps), that drives or entrains the brain waves for a naturally relaxed but attentive state, in which an easy flow of inner images can be observed.

In entheogenic ceremonies the role and significance of music, whether live or recorded, is enormously important and deserves to be attended to and planned with utmost care and consideration. Whether it is the chants of the *curandera* in the mushroom *velada,* or the *icaros* of the ayahuasca shaman, or the chants of the peyote *Roadman*, the melodies of the chant guide the voyagers through the other-worldly realms. The chants of the ayahuasca and mushroom shamans are sung with a soft, lilting rhythm – often with no words, just syllables or the names of spirits. They are invoking the particular spirits with whom that shaman is connected, imploring them to come and help with the healing, protecting and diagnostic seeing of the patients being treated. The peyote ceremonies of the NAC and related groups also use singing, accompanied by drumming.

One can observe that the peyote songs are typically accompanied by a fairly rapid drum beat, whereas the ayahuasca and mushroom chants have a slower and lilting rhythm. This may be a reflection of the fact that the mescaline and other alkaloids in peyote and related cacti are chemically in the phenethylamine family, which also contains the various amphetamines and tend to be more stimulating, as compared to the tryptamine derivatives DMT and psilocybin. In general, one can say that the repetitive rhythmic nature of the chants and songs provides essential support for the journeys through unfamiliar psychic territory. When one encounters fearful visions or painful memories, the rhythmic beat facilitates moving through the visions and reduces the likelihood of getting stuck in negativity, guilt or shame.

I remember on one of my early journeys with ayahuasca, I was listening to a recording of *icaros*, given to me by my friend, the anthropologist Luis Eduardo Luna, which he had recorded during a traditional ayahuasca healing ceremony. Unaccountably, as

I listened to the soft, warm voice of the healer, accompanied by occasional sighing and crying of a woman's voice, I became suffused with feelings of profound grief. After a while it dawned on me that my feelings were apparently being triggered by the *icaros*, and were not related to my life at all. When I asked Eduardo about that recording later, he told me that in that session the woman was being healed from the trauma of losing both her husband and her child in a violent incident. The healer's singing provided a soothing compassionate balm that accepted and uplifted the woman's tragedy – and this action even extended to a recording played at another time and place for other people. This is one factor that would lead one to prefer singing or other music that is individualized for the particular occasion.

Another incident that brought home to me the very practical value of having rhythmic music accompaniment was when I attend a ceremony of the *Santo Daime* church, where they not only sing strongly rhythmic hymns, accompanied by rattles and drums, but also move together in a simple two-step pattern, after drinking the ayahuasca tea. In those ceremonies, if you find yourself going through a painful experience, or you feel physically weak, you're encouraged just to step out and either sit or lie nearby. Usually someone will come and attend to you until you have gone through that rough spot in the flow of memories and visions. In this particular ceremony, I suddenly felt faint and near-nauseous and had to first sit and then lie down on the balcony right next to the room where the *Daime* dancing and singing ceremony was continuing. Suddenly I found myself apparently reliving a battle-field death scene from a past life, with blood, pain and gore. One of the healers came and did his hand movements on me and after maybe 10 or 15 minutes I felt better again. It was enormously significant for me that the dancing and singing continued uninterrupted in the room right next to me, where I could hear it and see it. It helped me not get caught up in the past-life trauma – but just see it as a tragic scene from some life long ago to which I had a recognizable but not persisting connection. In other words – the tragedy was over and I was alive and well.

In the memoir by Ram Dass and myself – *Birth of a Psychedelic Culture* – I related how surprised I was when I first encountered the California 1960s psychedelic scene in which hundreds or even thousands of people high on LSD or mushrooms were dancing to the music of The Grateful Dead or one of the other bands. As I was used to small group sessions with people lying in a circle listening to slow meditative music like Ravi Shankar, I could only imagine how chaotic and disturbing such mass-scenes would be. What I realized however was that in the "acid tests" and "raves" the continuous all-enveloping sound of the music provided a safe structure and container – in which people could dance and move, or sit quietly in contemplation. From time to time amid the dancers someone would sit on the floor, head bowed with some painful memories perhaps – a compassionate friend could usually be found, just sitting and holding them, until the stormy passage with grief and confusion had passed. The safe container of the music never stopped, through to the planned and gentle ending of the whole event.

In contemporary hybrid shamanic or entheogenic ceremonies it is typically the group leader who selects the music to be played, whether live or recorded. The selections may be made in accord with some specific criteria or intentions of the journey. As in the holotropic breathwork consciousness technology without drugs, developed by Stanislav and Christina Grof, different kinds of music may be selected for different phases of the journey. Because the influence of music in structuring the content of the experience is so profound it is best if there is an explicit agreement about how and by whom the music is selected.

I have been in leaderless groups where distressing arguments have erupted when the particular music selection triggered "bad trip" reactions and associations – leading to demands to "change the music." If there is an explicit agreement that one person selects the music to be played for the whole ceremony, then such disagreements over bad trip reactions, as well as disputes over what to play next, can be avoided or minimized. Then the individual with negative associations to the music can devote their attention to searching for the origin of these judgments and associations in their personal history, as well as practicing the non-judgmental mindfulness of a participant-observer.

On the other hand if the choice of music to be played is simply left to the discretion of whoever happens to have brought an audio player and recordings, without much explicit intention or prior agreement, this can lead to experiences of limited usefulness. I have been in sessions where the music played was predominantly loud and with insistent rock and even "heavy metal" rhythmic structures, due to the personal preferences of whoever provided the music player. This tended to induce a kind of passive attitude of just accepting, without much support for intentional exploration of novel inner spaces. The high-volume sounds themselves tend to mask or blot out more subtle auditory and synaesthetic perceptions. On the other hand, there are those groups and group leaders who purposely and preferentially use high-volume music with driving rhythms apparently believing that the person's defensive structures will be diminished in favor of access to supernatural or primal imagery.

In the groups in which I have been a participant-observer, we have found that the most favorable musical support for exploration and divination is music with a certain spaciousness in melodic, harmonic and rhythmic structure – that allows the explorer to follow the flowering and branching of associative streams of images and memories. For example, while slow adagio pieces by J. S. Bach are ideal for peaceful contemplation, his fast and complex contrapuntal pieces may engage too much of the left-brain analytic mind, and therefore tend to be avoided by entheogenic explorers. A second criterion we have found useful (somewhat at variance from the first) is to select music that is less familiar to typical Western audiences. There is an advantage in using music from other cultures, in which the typical Western listener is less able to engage the left-brain analytical and associative mind. Since the aim, after all, is consciousness expansion, it makes sense to make use of the vastly expanded access to musical forms from other cultures that is now available via recordings. In the appendix to my book *Worlds Within and Worlds Beyond,* I provide a list of some of the artists and recordings we have found most inspiring and evocative in our divination journeys.

In the hybrid entheogenic rituals of contemporary culture some group have adopted a practice similar to that of the Native American Church, where participants may take turns around the circle and singing, sometimes accompanied by drumming or rattling. Sometimes only a selected number of individuals choose to sing, or play an instrument, or sing accompanied by drumming. Sometimes there may be a small group of experienced musicians who provide the live musical substrate for the entire journey. There is definitely a different, more "alive" feeling to entheogenic sessions accompanied by live musicians. On the other hand, carefully selected recordings in different styles may elicit a broader spectrum of visionary content.

7. *The council format and talking stick practice.* All the variations of hybrid entheogenic group rituals discussed so far have involved instrumental music or singing, live or recorded. A whole different set of considerations arises in relationship to talking during or in the ceremony. Although amplified psycholytic psychotherapy, as described above, does involve verbal interaction between therapist and client, in the majority of what I have been calling hybrid entheogenic group rituals, non-talking during the ceremony is preferred. The beginning and ending of the non-verbal core of the session or journey is clearly marked – which allows for verbalization during the preparations beforehand and integration afterwards.

The reasons for the non-talking practice or custom are obvious: the expansion of sensory, affective and imagistic forms of consciousness during a psychedelic experience involve primarily right-brain functions, and their attempted translation into verbal forms invariably require attentive effort and a kind of "bringing down" of the experience. During the period of expanded consciousness such attempts at verbal translation or recording are likely to short-circuit and limit the psychedelic effect. On the other hand in the aftermath of the experience, verbal integration, whether by written or spoken descriptions, as well as integration by painting or drawing, provide essential bridges back into one's normal or usual existence.

There is no way to know how many groups in the contemporary psychedelic underground scene, even when there is a commitment to enhancing psycho-spiritual growth practices with psychedelics, adhere to a no-talking ritual structure. I remember that in the earliest days of psychedelic explorations in our Harvard projects we did not understand this principle, and would have sessions with lively dialogue and conversation. In our conversational memoir *Birth of a Psychedelic Culture*, Ram Dass and I relate several examples of these early group sessions in which conversations between two or three people in the group conversations could lead to confusing or downright chaotic group sessions – although they could also be accompanied by healing insights and moments of great hilarity. Because auditory perception is so enormously enhanced and sensitized, if people speak quietly or in whispers with one another in a group session, there is the easy possibility of triggering paranoid "ideas of reference" in which the person may think "why are they whispering – maybe they're whispering about me." So, in general, the no-talking practice – during the demarcated ritual time-period – leads to more useful sessions.

This is one of the safety elements of a group psychedelic ritual structure that is best discussed beforehand and agreed to by all participants, particularly when there is no one clear leader or guide for the overall course of the journey. In the states of enormously heightened sensitivity and suggestibility that occur with psychedelics, this factor can make the crucial difference between a group set-and-setting that is supportive of inner healing explorations or one that leads to anxious withdrawal and paranoid defensiveness on the part of one or more participants.

The group ritual form known as "Council," usually with something like a "talking stick," is a practice that apparently originated in and/or was adopted from Native American groups and became popular in New Age circles during the 1980s. Variants of the practice were developed further in various environmental and political activist groups, where there is no one clear "leader" but an attempt is made to allow everyone to have an equal voice (and sometimes, equal vote). The essence of the ritual structure is that people sit in a circle and a stick, sometimes decorated with feathers, or another object such as a crystal, a stone or a knotted piece of rope, is passed around. Whoever holds the object speaks and all others listen – respectfully and attentively, without questions, discussions or responses. In many circles when one person has spoken, the others may simply say "Ho" or "Aho" as acknowledgement and the staff is passed to the next person. I have personally observed how due to the equal respect and attention that is accorded to everyone in the circle, even the most withdrawn, shy or inexperienced person can bring forth unexpected flowerings of participatory genius.

In the early 1990s I participated in several workshops and conferences with Joanna Macy and John Seed, both in the United States and in Australia. Joanna and John had developed a group learning workshop experience they called *Council of All Beings*, the purpose of which was to assist environmental activists and others to move beyond alienation and find new inspiration in experiential and spiritual connection with the Earth. Their work is described in the book *Thinking Like a Mountain: Toward a Council of All Beings*, as well as other publications. The practices in these workshops do not involve any use of mind-expanding substances whatsoever. However, my colleagues and I have found them extremely relevant and applicable to the council-circle formats with entheogens. The vision and need for new experiential and spiritual connections with the natural world has been emerging independently in many different individuals and groups around the world.

There are two variations of the Council process – each with its advantages and drawbacks. In the traditional Circle format, the talking stick or object is passed around and each person says what they want or need to say; and the object is then passed on to the next person. One drawback of this method is that some people who don't really have anything they want to or need to share then somehow feel a pressure, not an inspiration, to come up with something. This can be avoided by making the sharing optional and just passing the talking stick to the next person.

With the other format, which one could call *Council,* the talking stick or other object is placed or held in the center of the circle and whoever feels inspired or moved to speak then picks it up. This method is not quite as inclusive as the circle, but has the advantage that those who speak are intentionally choosing to speak because they have something to say, not just because it's expected of them. The council format for group meetings is used in far more and more diverse groups and communities than only those involved with psychedelics. *The Way of Council* by Jack Zimmerman and Virginia Coyle, gives a good overview of the various applications of this approach, applicable in communities, schools, business environments, therapeutic groups or family systems. In essence, *Council* is a practice of open, heartfelt expression and attentive, empathic listening.

Many if not most of the groups using psychedelics for spiritual inner exploration and healing have adopted a council format, in either one of its two variations, for their rituals. In the hybrid shamanic-therapeutic groups I am most familiar with, the council circle format is used both at the beginning, when people are relating their intentions and healing purposes and at the end where people are describing and relating what they learned and what they will integrate into their lives.

The circle or council ritual forms, in addition to their use for verbal sharing before and after the ceremony, may also be used during ceremonies that involve singing, chanting or playing a musical instrument such as a guitar. Especially when there are accomplished musicians in the group, this can provide a particularly affecting way of sharing and amplifying the visionary gifts and inspiration received during the session. One major advantage of using non-verbal singing or toning during a group ceremony is that it maintains the right-brain focus of the experience and postpones the return to normal left-brain function of verbal description until the main substance effect has worn off.

In the entheogenic group divination ceremonies that I have been involved with, the following combination has evolved as the most fruitful: during the session itself there are periods of time when the participants sit in circle in a meditative posture and may chant OM or practice non-verbal *toning* (open vowel sounds), either with or without the accompaniment of a tamboura or similar drone instrument. Such periods of upright sitting and toning alternate then with periods where the individuals lie down and pursue their individual interior healing journeys, supported by music and/or guided meditations. Then towards the latter and closing part of the ceremony there may be a round where people can sing, play an instrument or verbalize something of significance that they are "bringing back" from their journey.

8. *The role of the elder, leader or guide.* There exists a whole spectrum of possibilities of guidance, ranging from individual psychedelic psychotherapy within a medical/psychiatric framework, to lightly structured self-organizing group sessions of psychedelic explorers, to individual healing sessions with shamans using traditional plant medicines, to religious ceremonies with one of the Brazilian ayahuasca churches. In most traditional ceremonies, such as with ayahuasca, iboga or San Pedro, and in many contemporary hybrid-shamanic-therapeutic groups the group leader basically conducts the ceremony – deciding on the timing and other details

of the ritual, the disposition of the medicines, the verbal guidance, the choice of music, and the handling of disruptions or adverse reactions. The leader is presumed to have more experience in the conduct of ceremonies and is typically engaged, and paid, by the individual participants. One could make an analogy to the practice of engaging an experienced mountain or wilderness guide who knows the local terrain. He or she determines the routes taken, the precautions, the equipment needed, etc. He or she also provides the verbal and vocal guidance for the inner explorations of the participants.

Westerners who participate in ayahuasca ceremonies run by Amazonian *mestizo* shamans may find themselves with someone who doesn't speak or understand English, who simply passes out the medicine and sings his traditional icaro healing songs, and the ceremony is then over. Western-trained individuals who provide traditional ceremonies or what I have been calling hybrid shamanic-therapeutic circles for other Westerners typically will typically provide much more intensive preparation before the ceremony and integrative discussions afterwards.

During the past twenty years there has been an increase in Western countries in "ayahuasca tourism," where individuals and groups congregate in certain towns in Peru, Ecuador and Brazil, seeking ayahuasca sessions with a native guide. There have been enough reports by now in Western media of abusive and/or exploitative behavior on the part of some "guides," so that there is a growing understanding of the potential hazards in such situations. Ayahuasca sessions, as with other entheogens, are experiences of heightened receptivity and suggestibility that can lead to deeply meaningful and healing changes, but also make one vulnerable to exploitative manipulation, especially in relation to money and sexuality. The use of mind-altering plant substances like ayahuasca is minimally regulated and restricted in South American countries – but instead is a normal part of the mestizo urban culture and economy, including tourism.

My point here is not in any way to denigrate the honesty, integrity and professionalism of most indigenous and mestizo shamans in South America or anywhere else. There are corrupt and incompetent healers and therapists in every country and community, in the industrialized North as well as in the tropical Third World. It is the responsibility of those seeking out the services of a guide or healer to thoroughly inform themselves of the qualifications and competence of the healer they are engaging with and to do their own "due diligence" before entrusting their receptive psychic state to someone of whom they have very little direct knowledge.

This caution applies to Westerners functioning or posing as guides equally as to indigenous or South American shamans. Only recently, an American whom I had been counseling sought my advice as to whether he should participate in a week-end workshop with ayahuasca that was being offered, facilitated by another American and recommended by two of his friends. I suggested that since he was going to entrust his receptive psyche to someone in an unfamiliar experience, it would make sense to request a face-to-face meeting with this putative shaman, prior to the ceremony, just to get acquainted. My client did so and a week later reported that the group leader had reacted to his request with mockery – asking "what are you expecting, that I might have horns, ha ha?" Needless to say, my friend declined to participate in the offered ceremonial experience.

The key requirement for participants in an entheogenic ceremony, as with a wilderness or mountain exploration or individual psychotherapy, is that they need to be able to trust the guide or therapist with whom they are engaging – and if they don't, then first work on whatever it is, in them or in the guide, that blocks such trust. This kind of trust is not "blind trust," but informed trust that recognizes that ultimately you are yourself responsible for your own physical and psychological safety and integrity.

The amount and kind of guidance provided by the group leader or session organizer will vary tremendously, as indicated above in the overview of the main kinds of entheogenic practices found in contemporary Western countries. There are two main variations or possibilities: (1) one person, who is recognized and respected by the participants as an elder with the most experience with the particular medicine being used, basically conducts the ceremony and supervises the different elements, including the dispensing of the medicine; and (2) a group of self-selected individuals with roughly equal amounts of experience and expertise, agree on a ritual format with rotating specific roles, rather than one overall guide.

I have known of several such groups, both in the US and in Europe, who have adopted some such egalitarian framework, which places the greatest emphasis on individual responsibility and probably counteracts idealizing and self-aggrandizing tendencies in self-appointed "shamans." Michael Harner and other anthropologists who have studied shamanic cultures always emphasized that in traditional cultures shamans are not appointed or elected by anyone – they are chosen by the Spirits, often in an uncomfortable way involving hardship and illness, and more or less dragged to perform their function for the community in which they live.

9. *Egalitarian group structure with rotating leadership functions.* The closest traditional precedent for the more egalitarian model

described above is the traditional NAC peyote ceremony – in which there are four clearly defined roles, rather than one individual leader who directs and decides everything. The *Roadman* conducts the ceremony and its timing, the *Drummer* provides the all-important rhythmic support for the singing, the *Fire Man* maintains the fire in the center which provides the concentrative focus as well as being guardian of the entrance, and the *Water Woman* brings in the feminine, nurturing element for balance. In such a traditional ritual there is little room for individual variation – in fact the power of the ritual depends in large part on the exact performance of the prescribed ritual in the traditional way.

In self-organizing, egalitarian groups there is great variation in the time and attention devoted to preparatory ritual elements such as prayer-like or meditative invocation of the spirits and explicit statements of intentions. My informal and non-systematic observations suggest that the more attention is paid to these preparatory elements the more productive and satisfying the rituals are likely to be. For example, in groups consisting of friends whose ordinary lives include interactions with each other and their families – it can be a helpful preparatory practice to clear the air of any unresolved disagreements and exchange apologies as needed – so that lingering negativity does not infect the spirit of the inner journey.

In such self-organizing, egalitarian groups with rotating functions, there is usually a sharing of responsibilities, similar to the peyote circle gatherings. One person or family provides the place for the ceremony, which is typically held at night and is followed by sleep in the same place and some kind of integrative process and food sharing, either after the ceremony or sometimes the next morning. There is explicit and/or tacit agreement on the main elements: people sit and lie in chosen places, often in an approximate circle which allows everyone to see everyone equally; someone brings and administers the chosen medicine which is dispensed and ingested (drunk, eaten, injected, smoked or snuffed); someone provides for the music, either recorded or live, or both; and some variation of a talking stick ritual is used for periodic sharing of experiences. Three of these elements deserve special and careful consideration – the *dosing*, the *music* and the *talking stick* rounds.

The dispensing of the initial medicine is a pretty straightforward process, but the timing and dispensing of *booster doses* can make a big difference between productive and inharmonious sessions. Booster doses typically extend the length of the action of the medicine in the body-mind and thus if there is at-will taking of additional booster doses it will be that much more difficult to perform a closing ceremony after which most everyone moves to the different time-space mode of socializing and eating. Therefore experience and common sense suggests that there be one pre-agreed time after the initial dose, let's say roughly 1 hour, where a supplemental or booster dose is ingested by those who choose to, but not thereafter. The amount of the booster can also be a consideration, especially with ayahuasca and mushrooms, which involve raw food items, but also with substances in the form of tablets or injected liquids like ketamine.

In the section of this book on *Spirit Medicine Practices* (p. 77), I discuss the dose-related issues and the all-important distinction between the *effective dose* and the *dissociative dose*. To my mind, it is an important part of taking responsibility for one's own health and well-being, as well as consideration for others in a group ceremony and the larger community, that the individual be aware of and calibrate his or her own intake of these mind-expanding substances with sensitivity to these factors. For this reason also, I personally think that it is best if the dispensing of medicines and booster doses is carried out by one individual in the group who has chosen to either abstain altogether from taking any medicines or only takes a threshold amount, so that his or her normal judgment is not impaired. I have been in non-directed, leaderless groups where the choosing and taking of booster doses was at will, by people with obviously impaired judging functions – with resulting effects both unpleasant and unproductive of useful inner work. An alternative process to having one person stay "unaltered" would be to measure out the potential booster doses ahead of time and everyone agrees just to take the pre-measured portion.

What music is played, live or recorded and by whom, can also be a source of disagreements and distractions if not carefully planned. In the NAC peyote ceremonies there is one drummer who sees to the timing and structure of the ceremony and also supports individual singers. The contemporary self-directed, leaderless groups in which I have been a participant-observer, have also usually had one person (by rotation or agreement) organize the selection of recorded music to be played. If all agree that this person selects the recordings for this particular session, then this avoids pointless and distracting disagreements about whether some other music would be preferable at any given moment. When I have been in groups and I didn't particularly "like" the music – I used the opportunity to silently practice the Taoist mantra *for those who have no preferences for or against anything, the Way is as wide open as the World."* In time the music was changed to a different mode and my mood changed accordingly. So this is the advantage of leaving the selection of recordings to be played to one person in each ceremony, by agreement. *((((*

TALKING-STICK?

The use of some variation of the talking-stick or talking-stone ritual for sharing in entheogenic ceremonies has become fairly widespread, as noted above. In the leaderless or rotating guide groups I have participated in, there is an agreement that anyone can call for a round with the talking stick at any time and it will be honored by all. Participants pull themselves out of a prone position absorbed in their inner journey and sit facing the center of the circle. There may be a smudging with fragrant herbs or incense that is passed around and then the talking stick will be passed around. This can be an opportunity to share with friends something of the personal journey of healing and visioning that the person is experiencing. It is best if there is no questioning, interpreting or responding from the others, beyond an appreciative *HO* at the end of each sharing – as described above in relation to the Council group process. In some groups the individual may sing instead of talk, or play an instrument instead of talk and this can often produce truly inspired and inspiring "channeled" vocalizing, in which the entire group enters into an ecstatic state. For practicing musicians such sessions can yield valuable material if recorded – but it goes without saying that any recording of anything said or sung during a session must be made only with prior agreement of all concerned.

Concluding reflections

Some practitioners of entheogenic or psychedelic exploration in freely associating groups may object to these descriptions of common practices because they feel that any implied or expressed structure that limits self-expression or "free choice" is somehow contrary to the spirit of adventure and exploration. No doubt there is a core belief and value system in many explorers, myself included, that would question and resist received assumptions and instructions – especially in a context of spiritual practice. What I am describing as recommended practices is of course a personal judgment based on my observations. Each individual and group makes up their own set of agreed-upon structures for their entheogenic sessions. I do think it is pointless and unproductive to make a set of agreements, such as a talking stick ritual for verbal reporting, and then violate it based on a libertarian assumption of "free choice."

This may be the decisive factor between those individuals and groups who want to use mind-expanding drugs primarily for recreation and those committed to a shared practice of healing and visioning. The latter certainly does not preclude or exclude genuine "re-creation" and enjoyment. An analogy that I prefer might be a group of musicians who sometimes get together to practice a pre-determined piece that they are planning to perform together. And sometimes they might just get together to play and expand into new territory – but still, in doing so, adhere to some kind of shared agenda and directions, like improvising while agreeing to stay within a chosen key, or playing with pre-selected instruments.

p29 ELEMENTS of THERAPEUTIC SESSIONS.
· SET
· SETTING

Time for prep = Time for experience = Time for integ.

p30 THE STRUCTURE (9 elements)
1. CIRCLE
2. SPIRITS - open your mind to this
   · 4 Directions ⟩ align ∂ them
   · Place
   · Time
   · ANIMAL (envelop allies in each of the below)
      · Land
      · Sea   ⟩ Evolution,
      · Reptiles   Adaptation
      · Birds
      · Insects

   PLANTS & FUNGUS → Interdependence
                      Food, Medicine,
   MINERALS & ELEMENTS   Beauty

   ANCESTORS / ELDERS
      → avoid judgement·

   DEITIES

p42 3. CLARIFY INTENTION
   (Intention → awareness)
         → Perception)
   · Intending (more focused
   · Asking (how open, gathering)

p43 4. ALTAR / TALISMAN / AMULETS
         Can focus the spiritual attention
p50 5. PRAYER / MUDRA → Hand positions.
p53 6. CHANTING / SINGING
         p58 → Type of music for exploration
p59 7. NON-VERBAL SILENCE / TALKING STICK
But chanting, etc... ↳ non-talking doing → agreement
         Integration → Talking Stick before you.
         p61, 62 1. CIRCLE
                  2. COUNCIL
p63 8. Role of the GUIDE / SHAMAN.
      p64 → Be careful the plants can
      make you vulnerable to exploitation
72
p66 9. EGALITARIAN STRUCTURE·

Two

Spirit Medicine Practices

The difference between the medicine and the poison is the dosage.
~Theophrastus Paracelsus

Sweet are the uses of adversity, which like the toad,
ugly and venomous, wears yet a precious jewel in his head.
~William Shakespeare

In 1964, when Leary, Metzner and Alpert wrote and published *The Psychedelic Experience,* as a guidebook using the Tibetan Book of the Dead, I was the one charged with writing the appendix on dosages, since I had just completed my post-doctoral fellowship in psycho pharmacology. We gave two sets of dosage ranges for LSD, mescaline and psilocybin – the three drugs that we were familiar with at the time. We had two columns: in column A we gave a "dosage sufficient for an inexperienced person to enter the transcendental worlds described in this manual" and in column B, "a smaller dosage to be used by more experienced persons or by participants in group sessions." For LSD we had 200-500 mcg (micrograms) in column A and 100-200 mcg in column B.[1]

---

1. I am indebted to David Presti, Ph.D., neurobiologist, cognitive scientist and clinical psychologist, who is on the faculty at UC Berkeley, for his careful reading of this and the next chapter. Any remaining errors are my own responsibility.

From the perspective of 50 years of experimentation and observation later, I would never make those kinds of dosage recommendations now. We had a wrong understanding of the inverted U-shaped dose-response curve with psychedelic drugs: the response of heightened perception-awareness rises initially with increasing dosages to an optimum level and then flips into dissociative and/or dysphoric responses (referred to colloquially as "body load" or "bad trip") as innate resistance and inhibitory factors are triggered. This is the principle expressed in the Paracelsus statement that "the difference between the medicine and the poison is the dosage." In other words, the safe and optimally useful dosage of any "medicine" is about midway between "not enough" and "too much."

Our group at Harvard were initially not aware of the relevance of alchemy, or shamanism, to psychedelic experimentation. The experimenters in Europe, like Hans-Carl Leuner and Stanislav Grof, who were working with the so-called "psycholytic" therapeutic approach of gradually increasing dosages in a series of sessions had, I now think, a better understanding of this principle. The point after all was not just to be "high," but to bring back useful content, in terms of healing and understanding, from one's excursions into expanded visions of reality. In a letter that Albert Hofmann wrote to Leary in response to the initial reports of the Harvard research, Hofmann expressed surprise, if not concern, at the high dosage levels we were working with in our studies with psilocybin.

Not only our group at Harvard, but also the vast majority of the psychedelic underground that grew up in the 1960s, the "hippie" movement starting in California – and I venture to say, some underground groups to this day – don't understand this principle, or they don't care about it. For them the operating motto seems to be "the more (or higher) the better." I remember conversations with the late Owsley Stanley, who reputedly manufactured millions of doses of high-quality LSD, that was liberally distributed at the "acid-test" dances, with non-stop rock music and thousands of revelers. He'd be pushing me and everybody around to take one of his tablets, that probably had 300-500 micrograms of LSD – almost like a kind of "dare." I always felt uncomfortable with that approach. But he made it sound like if you didn't take the higher dose, you're missing out on the real, cosmic thing.

There was an element of swagger to his attitude. Not to mention the fact that if you're taking dosages repeatedly over a period of days, resistance is built up and higher dosages are needed to feel any effect. And if your innate sensitivity is high, then a relatively lower dosage may already be a safe maximum for you.

However, I am not maligning in any way the enormous contribution Owsley and his chemist associates made to the cultural and social revolutions of the 1960s culture by manufacturing and distributing high-quality LSD, which was not illegal when they first started to produce it. Nor do I have any personal animus against him. He used to come bopping up to my house in Berkeley late at night, wake me up and insist on regaling me with his rants on everything from chemistry to cosmology and politics.

In the matter of dosages I also came to diverge from the similar opinions stated with flamboyant eloquence by my friend the late Terence McKenna, who used to say that in order to "really get the message" you have to take "heroic dosages." In *The Toad and The Jaguar*, I relate some explorations Terence and I did around this matter of dosages – and I do believe that his views mellowed somewhat in his later years. After all, the youthful years in all of us are time of exuberance and extremes, of breakthrough and experimentation.

My dosage statements quoted above (p. 73) from *The Psychedelic Experience*, show an incorrect understanding on our part of the meaning of "transcendence" and how it differs from "dissociation." I would not agree now with our quoted statement that the listed higher dosages of a psychedelic substance are "sufficient for an inexperienced person to enter the transcendental worlds." On the contrary, only those with prior long-term experience with meditation practices will likely be able to consciously enter transcendental realms, and then most likely with the lower dosages. One way to think of the difference is that *transcendence is conscious dissociation and dissociation is unconscious transcendence.*

A dosage so high that the effect cannot be assimilated, understood or described – for lack of a suitable language for one thing – is likely at best to result in a pleasant, maybe even blissful, experience, given a safe, supportive setting – but an experience from which little useful can be brought back and integrated. The psychedelic visionary expansions of consciousness are adversely affected if the dosage is too high to be assimilated by the body-mind complex – leading to unpleasant and/or dysphoric psychosomatic reactions overpowering any "insights" or "visions." Many, if not most, casual psychedelic explorations are likely to have some elements of both kinds of experience – an initial mostly dissociated phase, followed by potentially useful and partially remembered insights.

When the individual takes a dose higher than his dissociative threshold he or she will typically report just that it was "intense" or "far-out" but not be able to identify much content. Or the increased speed of mental associations may create paranoid or schizoid scenarios – which, fortunately in the vast majority of cases, if the setting is safe and protected, will diminish in intensity as the drug-effect wears off. I had an encounter a few years ago that brought home this point for me with the force of a revelation. A woman with quite a few experiences with psychedelics told me, with some pride, that she had taken "500 mikes of acid" last week-end, anticipating that I would be impressed. When I asked her about her experience, she could not describe or relate a single insight or vision from her five to six hour journey. It made me realize that such a dissociated experience was really a waste of time in this case – and in less protected and supportive settings could easily have led to a disaster in the form of a psychotic-like disorientation.

I doubt whether most of the easy-tripping flower children of the sixties or even the average person with sincere intentions for psychological growth who dabbled in psychedelics in the 1960s understood this dissociative dilemma. We didn't have the language for it – and still don't. I believe too that this may be one additional reason why many of the youthful trippers stopped taking psychedelics after a while. Experiences probably occurred that were either frightening or meaningless and draining of psychic energy – and there were not many psychotherapists experienced in these matters who could help them. It goes without saying that legal and social prohibitions probably also played a role in the decline of popular use.

Effective and dissociative/dysphoric dosage levels

In animal pharmacology research, it is customary to measure or estimate a minimally *effective dose* (ED-50) of a given substance, the level at which a response can be observed in 50% of the subjects; and a *lethal dose* (LD-50), the level at which 50% of the experimental animals die. The equivalent human toxic levels of that drug are then estimated by extrapolation, in relation to body weight. In the underground culture of psychoactive substance use, the danger of excessive dosages is not physiological collapse or death (as long as the drugs used are free of impurities), but psychological *dissociation*: unconsciousness of one's own bodily postures and gestures, vocalizations and verbalizations, as well as more or less total disconnect of awareness of one's surroundings.

In my book *MindSpace and TimeStream*, I pointed out that although psychedelic states are typically characterized by a vast increase in mental and visual associations, i.e. expansions of consciousness, dissociative and contracted states may occur with psychedelics if the dosage is too high for that individual, so that the amplified sensations and perceptions cannot be assimilated. "It is important to realize that dissociated drug states, involving a profound disconnect from time-space reality, are quite different than the classic psychosis-like 'bad trip' marked by confusion, high anxiety, strange sensations and distorted perceptions" (*op.cit.* p.105).

Dissociative experiences are those which cannot be meaningfully remembered or described – the person may simply notice afterwards that some time has elapsed and their memory is blank. Such dissociated experiences (or episodes within an experience) may not be accompanied by feelings of anxiety, and may not even be reported as "bad trips" by the person. There may be no feelings at all, or the person may report feeling calm or even blissful. To an outside observer there may be no visible behavioral changes. If the individual is in an unconscious dissociative state, observers may report the person uttering strange verbalizations or vocalizations and assuming unusual bodily positions or movements, of which the subject has no memory whatsoever. Such postural and vocal dissociative reactions can be alarming to others, though the persons themselves may report no discomfort or distress at the time, or afterwards.

"BAD TRIP" is different from a DISSOCIATIVE experience

Some drug experiences for some individuals, even in a safe, protected setting and with adequate preparation, may involve an intensity level that is described as "too much" – characterized by unpleasant, dysphoric, anxious sensations and feelings, that are typically described as a "bad trip," or more colloquially a "bummer," in the underground literature. Whatever mind-expanding insights may occur are overpowered by unpleasant psychosomatic symptoms – which typically wear off as the physiological drug effect in the body diminishes. It is not known what determines whether an excessive drug reaction will result in a dysphoric "bad trip" reaction or a dissociative disconnect.

In the following sections, my estimates of dosage ranges presuppose a safe, protected setting with adequate guidance and preparation, as well as a consistent degree of pharmaceutical purity. The basic understanding of the so-called "set and setting" model, first articulated by Leary in the writings of our group, implies that you can only meaningfully compare the effects of different drugs and dosages if you hold those factors constant. I will be quoting primarily from four different books on the chemistry of visionary hallucinogens. In the psycho-chemistry books by Alexander and Ann Shulgin (*PIHKAL* and *TIHKAL*) and by Daniel Trachsel (*Psychedelische Chemie*), as well as in Jonathan Ott's erudite compendium *Pharmacatheon,* all of them written more than forty years after the 1960s period of initial exploration with psychedelics, the comparison of different drugs is explicitly based on holding the set and setting factors approximately constant.

In particular, the Shulgins' comparisons of the psychological effects of a number of tryptamines and phenethylamines are based on a compilation of reports from his constant group of a dozen or so collaborators who met and compared observations of the

BOOKS ABT DOSAGES & EXPERIENCE

effects of a particular drug at different dosage levels – with the master chemist providing commentary on how these psychological observations correlated with differences in molecular structure. Shulgin used a four-point quantitative scale of subjective intensity and quotes from the qualitative descriptions by his collaborators. He describes the setting in which his group of associates met and the agreed-upon ground rules for behavior during the experiment, as well as the preparation beforehand and the integration period afterwards. Trachsel's book also quotes descriptions of the subjective drug effects at different dosages – although there is no indication or assumption that the set and setting are constant. Jonathan Ott's descriptions of the subjective effects of different plant, fungal or chemical substances are based exclusively on his own personal observations on himself, with a presumed constant set and setting.

The occurrence of dissociative experiences at higher dosages is not explicitly mentioned by these authors, but all give a dosage range for the substances they discuss, which implicitly acknowledges that there is an optimum for each substance, somewhere between "too little" and "too much." Reported experiences at dosages above the top of the range can clearly be discerned as being either dissociative and/or dysphoric.

I will be estimating the following two important dosage figures, based on the figures provided by these authors and my own observations in the underground psychedelic drug culture: *ED-50: the threshold dosage at which psychoactive effects are observed by about half the subjects, or in half the trials; and DD-50: the dosage at which about half the subjects, or half the experiences, involve some degree of dissociation and/or dysphoria.* Like the Shulgins and the other chemist authors I will also provide estimates of duration of effect – which generally, though not always, correlates with intensity.

Individual factors affecting intensity of experience

Besides the effective and dissociative/dysphoric dosage levels, there are three additional factors that can affect an individual's response to psychoactive substances: body weight, innate sensitivity and prior experience or learning. In the underground literature of drug experience reports, these factors are not generally assessed or reported. For a more complete understanding, they should always be considered.

Body weight. In medical pharmacology, dosage levels are customarily given in terms of mg per kg of body weight. The effective and dissociative dosages for a lighter person will be lower than that for a heavier person.

Innate sensitivity. There are inherent or innate differences in nervous system perceptual sensitivity – that are not easily recognized or measurable by any presently known medical or psychological instrumentation. At the high end of the sensitivity spectrum there are individuals, sometimes called clairvoyant or clairsentient, who respond more strongly and vividly than average to any perceptual stimuli, whether external or internal. Many artists and so-called psychics or intuitives fall into this category. The intensity of their perceptual and affective response to any given stimulus, internal or external, is stronger than average. Therefore the effective and dissociative dosage for them would tend to be lower than average.

This factor of innate individual differences in response sensitivity is not sufficiently appreciated in the underground drug sub-culture, according to my observations. A given dose of a drug can produce effects differing significantly in intensity in different individuals – even when the other factors of set and setting are held constant. I've come to believe such unrecognized individual differences in response sensitivity represent an additional factor that can lead to unpleasant and non-useful dissociative experiences in those who are focused solely on the specifics of the drugs ingested.

Experiential learning. In the groups I've observed, people seemed to learn through experience what their inherent sensitivity is and adjust their intake accordingly. Experienced inner space explorers and those who devote careful attention to the set and setting of their explorations will be far less likely to have dissociative elements in their experience than inexperienced and ill-prepared "trippers."

The range between the *ED-50* and the *DD-50* can be considered the level at which the average intelligent, well-informed, seeker-observer can expect to have psychologically useful and philosophically meaningful experiences. The estimates given here should be considered minimal preparatory information for the average person. I am basing my dosage range estimates on my observations in the underground drug culture over the past 50 years, as well as on the statements in the chemistry handbooks by the Shulgins, Trachsel and Ott. An additional source of information on dosages is the *Erowid* website, giving more details from underground informants of the kinds of experiences that can be expected from psychoactive substances at different dosages.

Such dosage estimates can only be meaningfully given for purified drug substances. For the user of plant or fungal materials, whether raw or cooked, the concentrations of the psychoactive principle can obviously vary enormously. "Due diligence" is always necessary in informing oneself beforehand, not afterwards, on the presumed potency of the medicine ingested.

In what follows, I will also be quoting short extracts from the three poetic ethnobotanical treatises by Dale Pendell – *Pharmako/Poeia, Pharmako/Dynamis* and *Pharmako/Gnosis*. I am grateful to Dale for allowing me to use these brilliant guidebooks to the boundary-crossing, mind-expanding, creativity-enhancing potentials of these remarkable plants and fungi.

LSD – Lysergic acid diethylamide

ED-50 : 50 mcg
DD-50 : 200 mcg
6 - 8 HRS

This is the most famous and infamous of psychoactive drugs, praised and cursed, revered and reviled. It has been called "emperor of medicines," because of its supreme potency, but also "the medicine of emperors," because of its extraordinary range of powerful mind-expanding effects. The story of Albert Hofmann's serendipitous discovery of LSD and subsequent thousand-mile bicycle ride, has entered into scientific-cultural and pop-cultural history. Dozens of books and thousands of articles, both scientific and journalistic, have been written about this substance.

Shulgin gives 60-200 micrograms, and Trachsel 50-200 micrograms as the effective dosage range and Ott suggests a wider effective range of 50-500 mcg. Though these authors do not explicitly give the likelihood of dissociative responses as the reason for the upper level – it may be assumed that dosages above 200mcg are likely to be largely dissociative and/or dysphoric for most people. As mentioned above, the dose of 500 mcg, which became almost a kind of benchmark of hipness in the free-wheeling 1960s, is more than double the upper end of the currently recommended range.

My own dosage estimates for the most productive experiences are similar: *50 mcg for the ED-50 and 200mcg for the DD-50.* Duration: 6- 8 hours. It has been pointed out that the wide-spread street-use of higher dosages (above 200 mcg) of LSD declined precipitously in the late 1960s, due in part to more limited availability, as well as a number of sensational criminal cases associated with LSD use, and the criminalization of its use and manufacture. So there seemed to be a kind of social self-correcting process – in which the use of doses in the range of 75-200 mcg became more common.

Dale Pendell describes LSD in *Pharmakognosis*, in a section on *Phantastica*, in a chapter titled *The Luminosity of Sentient Dimensions* (pp. 59-72).

> For Modernism, birthed in African masks and absinthe and the Great War, LSD was the Grail. Alterity. Abstraction. The transgressor of boundaries. A sacrament looking for a context.

> Poison or medicine. Acid as the dogma dissolver. The universal solvent. Antecedents vanishing. 'It' just becomes its own antecedent. It has no antecedent. A clear slate. It's not "getting rid of the ego" either, just listen to the blow-hards who talk that way. More a clarifying and strengthening, a letting go that lets it emerge more freely.

> Wandering. Bardo. "The winds of karma". Shape-shifting. Face, mirror-work. Dissolve. Other faces, teachers, "my precursors."

> We used to say, if someone started crying, "she is having a religious experience." Tears were the mark. Tears of compassion. Tears for all the pain swirling in the world. And tears for the stark, underlying, eternal beauty and love shining at the core of all creation, fabulous, told in tales, yet truer than our cynicism.

An interesting practice that has emerged in the last 10 to 15 years, is the use of micro-doses of LSD, in the range of 50 micrograms or less (40, 30, 20). I have heard Albert Hofmann declare that he himself experimented with extreme low dosages, as low as 10 mcg – not for a distinct altered state, but "just to think". There are underground stories of experienced high-performance athletes taking micro-doses while rock-climbing, skiing, sky-diving or scuba-diving. This may be an area that will find more applications in future times. James Oroc has written a little about this topic, which seems to have been kept secret by tacit agreement.

There is an additional unusual effect of LSD that I have observed that has not, to my knowledge, been reported in the literature: in a small but definite and unpredictable number of people the effects of one dose of LSD (which normally lasts from 6-8 hours) may last for 24 to 36 or more hours, with undiminished intensity. This was brought home to me in a therapeutic session I conducted with a young woman some years ago. She supplied her own LSD from a presumed reliable source and the dosage she took was moderate, around 150-175 mcg. The setting was her own home, where she felt safe and comfortable, with only her mother also present. As an aspiring musician, her intentions were to explore the sources and possible extensions of her creative impulse. I stayed with her for about 5-6 hours, exploring family issues we had worked on before in therapy. She had some good insights, and spent some time at her piano ¬ her experience was productive, if not especially dramatic. After about five hours, when it became time for me to leave, she reported that the physical intensity of her body response was not diminished – but she felt fine and safe. I left and called her later that evening (the session had been during the daytime), about 7-8 hours after ingestion – and she reported that she was fine, but not at all tired or sleepy, and the effects were continuing at the same intensity. We talked again the next morning – the effects were continuing, and the next afternoon, when they gradually diminished allowing her to sleep.

This experience was very revealing to me: I realized that the occurrence of unexpected and unpredictably extended trips could explain some major disasters that have occurred. What if someone, expecting a six hour trip, took LSD on a week-end and then was still tripping strongly when it came time to go to work on Monday morning, or go home to family, or find their way through city streets? Paranoid delusions of permanent brain-damage would spring naturally to mind if the possibility of this kind of extended, though ultimately finite duration trip was not known or appreciated.

150 → 350 mg
8 - 10 hour.

Mescaline – 3,4,5-trimethoxyphenethylamine

This is the longest-known classical hallucinogen, having been isolated from the peyote cactus by the German chemist Arthur Heffter in the 1890s. Long before LSD was discovered, there were studies conducted at the University of Heidelberg in the late 1920s and early 30s, by Kurt Beringer and others. Timothy Leary and I suggested, in an article in *The Psychedelic Review* in 1965, that the novelist Hermann Hesse might have been a participant in those studies, since several of his novels, especially *Steppenwolf* and *Journey to the East*, seemed to contain disguised descriptions of psychedelic experiences. This suggestion was strenuously denied by the Hesse family heirs – although they no doubt enjoyed the renewed attention and sales of their father's writings.

It was mescaline that Aldous Huxley took, with the guidance of psychiatrist Humphrey Osmond, which inspired him to write his seminal book *The Doors of Perception,* in 1954. The phrase "doors of perception" itself came from William Blake's visionary poem: "If the doors of perception were cleansed, everything would appear as it is – infinite." Huxley wrote that this cleansing or open-ing of the windows or doors was a "gratuitous grace" – in other words, not a guaranteed "drug effect."

In *The Psychedelic Experience*, we gave 600-800 mg as the dosage for transcendental experiences, an amount that I would now consider likely to lead to dissociative experiences; and 300-500 mg as the dosage for "experienced persons." The *Erowid* site lists 200-300 mg as a "common" dosage and 300-500 mg as a "strong dose." Both Shulgin and Trachsel give a range of 200-400 mg – with slight variations on whether the hydrochloride or sulfate extract is used. Jonathan Ott gives 150-1000 as a dose range, though, as with LSD, the high end of his range far exceeds what I estimate to be the dissociative threshold.

My estimates are that *150-350 mg represents the range between the ED-50 and DD-50.* Duration: 8-10 hours. [2]

PEYOTE> SAN PEDRO

Peyote and San Pedro cacti

Mescaline is the primary, though not the only psychoactive component of the ground-hugging button-like peyote cactus (*Lophophora williamsii*) as well as the columnar San Pedro cactus – *Trichocereus pachanoi* and *Trichocereus peruvianus* having the highest concentrations. Different species and varieties will vary considerably in the concentration of mescaline – so no common standard figures can be given, although in general the concentrations of mescaline in the peyote cactus is perhaps ten times that in the San Pedro cactus, i.e. the San Pedro is less potent. In the peyote ceremonies of the Native American Church, participants consume

---

2 Mescaline dosages are measured in milligrams, and LSD dosages in micrograms. I mg is equivalent to 1000 mcg. Thus LSD is almost a thousand times more potent than mescaline; though they are equally "powerful," i.e. can elicit the same intensity of response.

Jonathan Ott has stated that pure synthetic mescaline has virtually disappeared from the black market, because of the price. Black market "mescaline" is very likely to be disguised LSD. A typical dose of 500 mg mescaline would cost about $125. For the reason of greater potency, LSD is a much more marketable commodity. Mescaline is much more likely to consumed in the form of its plant sources – peyote or San Pedro cactus.

about a handful of the cactus material, probably containing about 300-500 mg of mescaline. According to analyses by the independent botanist-chemist K. Trout, *Trichocereus pachanoi* yield a range of 25-120 mg mescaline per 100 grams of fresh cactus, which is high variability. The more potent species *Trichocereus peruvianus* contains as much as 80 mg mescaline per 100 grams of fresh cactus.

The market for the peyote cactus is under some pressure because it is a recognized legitimate sacrament of the Native American Church (NAC) in the US. In Mexico it is the central sacrament of the Huichol Indians. Dale Pendell, in *Pharmakognosis* gives a good account of the three main strands of the peyote story: through Mexico with the Huichol and the Tarahumara; through the rest of North America with the Native American Church; and through the European tradition via mescaline. He describes the preparatory ritual set-up of a NAC ceremony –

> Anyone who has ever participated in a Zen sesshin would feel very much at home – the careful sweeping of the sacred space, the discussions among the leaders on the minutiae of the ceremony – which side of the flap do people exit after the water ceremony, does the main prayer follow or precede the cedarman's prayer, etc. Bundles of willow twigs marked the inner perimeter, and sprigs of sage that had been tied together lay in a radial pattern around the edge of the tipi. The wood, mostly maple, was carefully stacked outside the entrance. The sun was setting and we awaited the roadman (*op.cit.* pp. 98-99).

There are five main ceremonial roles in the classic NAC peyote ritual: the _Roadman_ who conducts the ceremony; the _Cedarman_ who handles the smudging with purifying cedar smoke; the _Drummer_ who moves around the circle, supporting each singer in turn with his water-drum; the _Fire Man_ who tends the blazing fire in the center of the tipi and monitors who leaves to attend to bathroom needs; and the _Water Woman_, who comes at dawn to bring fresh water for everyone to drink. The songs in the peyote ceremony are not story-songs or ballads as we may think of them – they are inspired prayer chants, sometimes syllables only, that the individual has received from the spirits, praying for healing, for vision, for peace in the family or the community.

> Have you come full circle now? So that you can pray with us who have sat up all night here eating peyote? Will you be here when the water-woman enters in the morning? When this water-woman, as beautiful as the Goddess of Mercy, enters at dawn with food and water, when she takes your hand and wishes you the first "Good Morning" of your new life? (Pendell, D. _op.cit._ p. 115)

In the traditional ceremonies with San Pedro, called _cuchuma_ in the Bolivian and Peruvian highlands, the whole cactus is cooked for hours in a large communal pot – and one foot-length/hand-width amount of plant material is considered an amount for one person's night-time journey. The concentration of mescaline in this cactus is much less than in peyote. However, it has the advantage of easy cultivation and rapid growth. As Jonathan Ott points out, the seeds of the San Pedro cactus contain no mescaline and are thus legal. It can also be grown from cuttings – and is in fact a common ornamental cactus in many areas of the American Southwest and of course in Mexico. It has also been prepared as a concentrated concoction, or cooked in pressure cooker, which greatly reduces the necessary cooking time. Pieces of the cactus can also be nibbled fresh, "like eating a somewhat bitter cucumber" according to Dale Pendell.

> In an hour I could feel the medicine pulsing through me. I left the group and started walking into the wind, towards the sun. A special sparkle in the sand. Mescaline sparkle. Undulating ribbons of sand moved towards me across the beach…

It's the wind, the chill when the sun sets. We huddle. Homo sapiens, the huddling species. We huddle, talk some funny things, share visions – a kite becomes a hummer, an opening, a hole through this world to another. Or we moan, the mescaline sending waves of energy up and down our spines, orgasmic waves and shudders and evocations, and all of lying together, holding, burrowing for warmth, comfort – this primal craving, deeper than sex, that we so rarely satisfy. It is our answer to the great chill, to death, to the infinity of space (*op.cit.* p. 124).

A non-altered state use of San Pedro cactus has arisen in some segments of the US and European entheogenic underground. First the skin of the San Pedro cactus (which contains the psychoactive alkaloids) is cut off and dried. It can be stored dry indefinitely without loss of potency. It is then ground into a fine powder, straining out the remains of the spikes. A full-blown mescaline dose could be obtained from this powder if it were mixed into a kind of slurry – but because the mescaline content in the San Pedro cactus skin is only about 1-2%, one would have to consume 20-40 grams of the dried powder in this slurry – a difficult, if not impossible proposition. A variant use pattern has however developed in the US underground: the dried cactus skin powder is encapsulated in size 00 caps – and 1 – 3 capsules can be consumed and provide a "walking-around" enhanced level of awareness.

At this level, there are no closed eye hallucinations, or open eye visual changes, as there would be with a full dose mescaline trip. One can function and concentrate on external tasks and notice no difference. The best and most interesting use of this mildly psychoactive powder comes from walking around in nature: there is a noticeable enhancement of visual depth and color perception, positive mood and strength of concentrative meditation. The effect is extended after a couple of hours by eating some protein-containing food, which seems to re-activate it. This cactus powder is also consumed in some group ceremonies together with a dose of MDMA – where it seems to provide a kind of organic plant-based substrate, containing multiple different alkaloids, to the synthesized and purified phenethylamine.

Ibogaine and Tabernanthe iboga

200 – 500 mg
5 – 7 hours

Preparations made from the bark of the roots of this tropical shrub play a major role in the initiatory and healing rituals of the Bwiti cult in equatorial Africa (Zaire, Congo). The death of the old self and rebirth of a new and healthier self are underlying themes of these rituals, which involve consuming enormous quantities of a mush containing the ground-up root of *iboga* or *eboka*. The rituals, whether adolescent initiations or curative ceremonies, can go on for three days and involve a whole village or extended family, the initiate being supported, bathed and ceremonially painted by older members of the cult, while drummers, musicians and dancers keep up a non-stop accompaniment. I learned a lot about the uses of *iboga* (or *eboka*) in Gabon from the Italian anthropologist Giorgio Samorini, who was one of the first Westerners to be initiated into the Bwiti cult, in the 1960s.

Semi-synthetic and totally synthetic extracts of ibogaine were used as adjuncts to psychotherapy in the 1960s, by Claudio Naranjo, Leo Zeff, Jack Downing and some other psychotherapists including myself in the later 1960s. The doses used in these psychotherapeutic sessions in the 1960s were much less than those used in the addiction treatments described below. Their duration was similar to a moderate dose of LSD or mescaline – i.e. five to seven hours. *The dosage range of these moderate, therapeutically valuable ibogaine sessions I would estimate as 200-500 mg, i.e. comparable to mescaline.* Shulgin gives "hundreds of milligrams, up to one gram" as the effective dose range; Trachsel 200-1000mg. Both emphasize the vegetative distress symptoms and anxiety that can accompany the trip in the initial stages – although I do not remember these as being significant at the low to moderate doses we were using.

In the experiments I participated in the 1960s I was impressed by the potential of ibogaine enhanced psychotherapy. In contrast to the classical kaleidoscopic and fractal imagery with personal associations and a roller-coaster of emotions found with mescaline, LSD or psilocybin, the ibogaine trip had an assertively objective yet totally non-judgmental quality. Acquaintances of mine referred to the spirit of this medicine as clearly masculine, as "Mr. Iboga." Indeed, in one of my journeys I encountered this Spirit-Teacher as an African man wearing a slouch hat, who seemed to have a blend of African and mythic Nordic features, and who showed me some valuable insights about myself. You could find yourself impartially observing film-like scenes from your childhood, as if through a kind of *memory-scope*. You could observe your emotions and behavior with a detached yet compassionate attitude – and with the definite feeling that you could make different, healthier choices, with better outcomes.

In recent years, synthetic ibogaine has found a use in the treatment of addiction, administered in residential treatment centers in Canada, Mexico, Holland, Thailand and other places. These centers use ibogaine to treat all kinds of substance addictions, including heroin, alcohol, cocaine, methamphetamine, methadone, oxycontin. The treatment centers typically offer a comprehensive detox and therapy program, with extensive preparation and follow-up, under medical supervision. Typical doses of ibogaine administered in these addiction/withdrawal programs are 12-24 mg/kg, which is much higher than the "psychedelic" doses used in the 1960s or in the underground. The treatments require strict medical supervision because of the potential of death during an opiate withdrawal phase. Findings indicate that the characteristic opiate withdrawal symptoms are often completely gone for up to 5 to 6 days or more – giving the addict an important fore-taste and reminder of being free of their addiction. Two documentary films have appeared in recent years, providing dramatic and inspiring footage both of the indigenous ceremonies of the Bwiti cult and the use of ibogaine in addiction treatment: *Ibogaine – Rite of Passage*, by Ben de Loenen (2004); and *I'm Dangerous with Love*, by Michael Negroponte (2010).

(Probably 5mg/1g of dried Stropharia cubensis)
10-25mg

Psilocybe mushrooms and psilocybin
3-6 hr.

Timothy Leary had his initiatory vision experience with *psilocybe* mushrooms, *hongos alucinantes* as they were referred to in the local press, while on a vacation trip in Mexico, and initiated the Harvard studies in the Fall of 1960. As good fortune would have it, the active principle *psilocybin* had been recently identified by Albert Hofmann, and was made available by Sandoz pharmaceuticals to Leary, who with colleagues initiated a series of research projects. I was one of the graduate students participating in these studies. I concentrated on a study with Concord prison inmates, to determine if the psilocybin-induced visionary experience would promote behavior change, including lowering the recidivism rate. All of my initial experiences and the various research projects we did during the first year at Harvard were with synthetic psilocybin, in the form of little tablets from Sandoz pharmaceuticals. After Harvard closed down the research project, none of us anymore had

Connected o oratory, origin of language.

93

any contact with synthetic psilocybin since that time. Recently, a volume of the collected research papers from the early studies with psilocybin and LSD, collected and edited by culture studies professor James Penner, has appeared, titled *Timothy Leary – The Harvard Years*.

In *The Psychedelic Experience*, the dosage range we gave for psilocybin in the "A" column was 40-60 mg, which I would now consider a dangerous overdose. In fact one of the worst psychotic trips of my life, when I came close to suicide, as I described in *Birth of a Psychedelic Culture*, occurred with a dose of 60 mg. In *The Psychedelic Experience*, in the "B" column, for experienced users, we listed 20-30 mg, which I would still consider on the high end. Shulgin gives 10-20 mg; Trachsel 8-25 mg; Torsten Passie, a German researcher, provides three levels in a total range of 10-35 mg; Ott gives 5-50 mg, again stretching the high end.

My own current estimate of the dosage range for psilocybin is between an *ED-50 of 10 mg and a DD-50 of 25 mg*. The duration of a psilocybin or mushroom experience is 3-6 hours, i.e. about half that of LSD or mescaline trips. As a rough guide to the effective dosage ranges of psilocybe mushrooms, Jonathan Ott estimates that 5 grams of dried *Stropharia cubensis*, the most commonly found species, contains 25 mgs of psilocybin – so the *ED-50 of those mushrooms would be 2 grams and the DD-50 would be 5 grams*. The potency of different mushroom samples varies greatly and the responsible user will exercise the appropriate preliminary research and caution.

There is cross-tolerance between all three drugs (LSD, mescaline and psilocybin) – meaning there is a refractory period of about 24 – 36 hours after ingestion of one of these drugs, in which the response intensity to one of the others is reduced by about 50%.

Apart from the duration, most people would consider the perceptual and psychological effects and spiritual potentials of these three substances to be virtually identical.

In recent government sanctioned research projects, psilocybin has been studied for the relief of end-of-life anxiety by Charles Grob, MD and in the induction of mystical experience by Roland Griffiths, MD – the latter being a more carefully controlled replication of the famous "Good Friday" study carried out by Walter Pahnke, MD in the 1960s. Very recently, brain imaging studies of volunteers who had taken psilocybin, produced some very interesting findings related to the idea of consciousness expansion. These studies with fMRI (functional Magnetic Resonance Imaging) measurement, carried out at Imperial College London under the direction of David Nutt, showed *decreased blood-flow* in "hub" areas of the brain concerned with functional inter-connectivity and concepts of "self" and "ego." This finding is consistent with the notion that psychedelics like psilocybin reduce or suspend the normal functional filtering activity of the brain, what Aldous Huxley had metaphorically called the "reducing valve."

As far as the psychedelic underground is concerned, pharmaceutical psilocybin, like pharmaceutical mescaline, appears to be essentially unavailable. As with the history of mescaline, peyote and San Pedro, the illegalization of the drug stimulated the underground search for wild and cultivated products that contain the psychoactive essence – and coincidentally led to the re-discovery of traditional, indigenous uses of these substances.

In a 1957 *Life Magazine* article, R. Gordon Wasson, the ethnomycologist-banker, revealed the survival of traditional pre-Conquest Mexican mushroom cults in remote villages in Oaxaca. There followed somewhat of an unwanted deluge of hippie tourists for several years, descending on Mexican mountain villages in search of these traditionally sacred entheogenic fungi. More and more varieties and species of psilocybin-containing mushrooms have been identified, in the Pacific Northwest especially, but also in Hawaii, Europe, Australia, Indonesia, Bali, Thailand and elsewhere. In 1976, the McKenna brothers, under the pseudonyms O.T. Oss and O.N. Oeric, produced the first booklet describing an indoor, high-yield *psilocybe* mushroom cultivating method.

Psilocybin and psilocin are naturally occurring psychedelics with a long history of human use. Both are present in 'psychedelic' or 'magic' mushrooms. Psilocybin, the better known of these two chemicals, is metabolized after ingestion into psilocin, which is the primary active chemical. Paul Stamets, author of the definitive guide *Psilocybin Mushroom Species of the World* (1996) states there may be as many as 100 different psychoactive species, most of them in the genus *Psilocybe*, which has eighty species as well as the genera *Panaeolus, Pluteus, Conocybe* and others. Considerable variation in psilocybin content of the various species is of course found. Stamets gives a table showing the % psilocybin in a dozen different species. In decreasing order of potency the first six are: *P. azurescens, P. bohemica, P. semilanceata, P. baeocystis, P. cyanescens, P. tampanensis* and *P. cubensis*. In the visionary mushroom underground culture, the mushrooms are usually dried and stored, and then reactivated with water; sometimes eaten with chocolate, which was apparently the traditional Aztec method.

Dale Pendell writes about *The Genus Psilocybe: Teonanácatl,* high-lighting the oft-observed connection between psilocybe mushroom experiences and the nature and origin of language, especially oracular poetry.

An Edenic pre-human wisdom, locked away, stashed in ancient life-forms, like scrolls hidden in a cave. Or like angels of an archaic race of gods, whose temples are part of mind, whose foundations have seen countless cities and empires rise and fall.

And now I know, I too know. I who have heard your cry, I who have voiced your wailing, now I know where words come from, now I know where language begins, now I know what real worlds sound like, and now I know what keening is – and now I know why we walk upright and why we leave offerings (Pendell, D. *Pharmakognosis*, pp. 33-37).

Ayahuasca or yajé

Ayahuasca is an hallucinogenic Amazonian plant concoction that has been used by native Indian and mestizo shamans in Peru, Colombia and Ecuador for healing and divination for hundreds, perhaps thousands of years. It is known by various names in the different tribes, including *caapi, natema, mihi* and *yajé*. The name *ayahuasca* is from the Quechua language: *huasca* means "vine" or "liana" and *aya* means "souls" or "dead people" or "spirits." Thus "vine of the dead," "vine of the souls" or "vine of the spirits" would all be appropriate English translations. It is however slightly misleading as a name, since the vine *Banisteriopsis caapi* is only one of two essential ingredients in the hallucinogenic brew, the other one being the leafy plant *Psychotria viridis*, which contains dimethyltryptamine (DMT). But DMT is not orally active, being metabolized by the stomach enzyme monoamine oxidase (MAO). Certain chemicals in the vine inhibit the action of MAO and are therefore referred to as MAO-inhibitors – their presence in the brew makes the psychoactive principle available and allows it to circulate through the bloodstream into the brain, where it triggers the visionary access to otherworldly realms and beings – which can typically last 4-5 hours.

Besides its use in South American *mestizo* shamanism, ayahuasca has also migrated into urban populations in Brazil, where it has became the central ceremony for two religious movements – the UDV (*Uniao do Vegetal*) and the *Santo Daime* – through which several hundred people participate in ayahuasca drinking once or twice a month, in Brazil alone. In addition, these folk-religions have won adherents and congregations in several European countries and the United States. So it can be safely stated that ayahuasca is the most widely consumed hallucinogen in the world today.

Jonathan Ott, in *Ayahuasca Analogues* (1994), his review of studies of ayahuasca and its various admixtures, cites four different chemical analyses of ayahuasca samples, which found that the average amount of DMT in the admixtures was 29 mg. Such a dose is comparable to the low end of the range for smoked DMT, but lasting four to five hours, instead of 5-10 minutes. The absorption of DMT via the admixture in potions of ayahuasca is clearly more efficient than when it is smoked—exemplifying the principle of "doing more with less." The percentage of DMT in the five different samples of ayahuasca varied from 0.1 to 1.46, with an average 0. 68.

In my edited collection of original essays *Ayahuasca – Sacred Vine of Visions,* (2013) neurochemist J. C. Callaway points out:

> "under ordinary circumstances DMT is rapidly metabolized by MAO, the same enzyme that metabolizes serotonin.... After MAO is inhibited by harmala alkaloids, DMT becomes orally active and intricate visual displays of colored patterns are often achieved through this combination....It is worth noting that the effects from orally activated DMT are qualitatively different from either smoked or injected

> DMT in the absence of MAO inhibition....When smoked
> or injected, DMT seems to have all the cognitive content of
> a fireworks display"(*op.cit.* pp. 106-107).

Callaway, in his analysis of twenty samples of the hoasca tea used
in the UDV, reported an average DMT content of 36 mg per dose,
with a range of 29-43 mg.

The key to the remarkably curative and therapeutic visions in a
typical ayahuasca experience seems to be its effect on brain levels of
the neurotransmitter *serotonin,* or *5-hydroxytryptamine.* Deficiency
in basic serotonin levels has been implicated in conditions in
depression, anxiety, irritability, violence, insomnia and a number
of psychosomatic conditions. Serotonin is normally metabolized
in the body by the MAO enzyme, and so the MAO-inhibiting
substance leads to an increase in endogenous serotonin levels of the
brain, lasting at least the four to five hours of a typical ayahuasca
experience. The heightened serotonin levels may account for the
fact that ayahuasca takers are often remarkably calm and unafraid
of the seemingly terrifying visions they are confronting.

Serotonin is also present in the intestines where it increases
intestinal motility, and at higher levels can induce vomiting and/
or diarrhea. These are the basis for the purging action of ayahuasca,
which is known among some of the *mestizo* healers as *la purga.*
These traditional healers usually recommend or require (depending on the strictness of their adherence to tradition) a severely
reduced-protein and simple carbohydrate diet in preparation for
the ayahuasca ceremony. As many of the accounts in my collection of ayahuasca experiences attest, the purgation that typically
accompanies an ayahuasca experience is actually not experienced
as a symptom of an existing sickness, as it would be normally, but
rather as a welcome release of the toxic residues of the person's

rience in contemporary industrial society.

... Pendell, in *Pharmakognosis*, writes of his ayahuasca visions–

The first thing I learned was that ayahuasca is not a plant at all. It is a very large snake, a boa, that lives under the water. The boa loosened her coils and after a while I could breathe again, like ordinary people. She coughed up some phlegm and told me to swallow it. Even this I did. But it was only when her teeth were on my neck that I could sing.

There were many iridescent women there – iridescent girls grinding corn with the peccary women, making *chichu*. The boa swam towards me and swallowed me. Inside was like a cave, where the ribs of the boa were sparkling stalactites.

The vine is the Queen of Medicines. It is the vine that produces the forms. We add the leaves to give them light.

I saw the origin of the universe go into the vomit basin, in colors that I'd never before seen. Enough! Be gone ten thousand sufferings. The ills of the world and my own ills. All the ignorance and greed and fear, all the self-centered protections that hurt everyone and make it all worse (*op.cit.* pp. 141-154).

No general guidelines as to dosages of ayahuasca can be given of course – since it is a brew that is prepared on site, by the group guide or church functionary, according to their beliefs, training and experience. It is therefore highly recommended that potential participants in a ceremony inform themselves thoroughly beforehand about the qualifications and prior experience of the person who is providing the ayahuasca medicine. Ayahuasca is a folk-medicine in several South American countries, and tourists can buy bottles of it from street vendors (a practice with obvious dangers).

Even experienced local and Western medicine providers can make mistakes in preparation of the brew. I experienced this once to my regret when I participated in a ceremony in which the ayahuasca brew (for which a normal dose usually involves drinking a small cup of the liquid) had been extremely concentrated (for ease of travel) into a form in which a standard dose consisted of a table-spoon of the liquid. When I requested an additional booster because the initial effect was sub-threshold, I was given an additional half-table-spoon, which precipitated me into a dissociated state lasting several hours – from which I remembered neither my experience nor my apparently disruptive vocalizations. My companions actually removed me to another room to shut me up – a maneuver of which I had absolutely no memory. Although the experience didn't leave any lasting negative effects in me, I considered my behavior, for which I apologized, completely inappropriate, and that of the medicine-maker a foolish experiment – for which he apologized.

Jurema and Mimosa tenuiflora

Mimosa tenuiflora (aka *Mimosa hostilis*) is the name of a shrub or tree native to NE Brazil and southern Mexico. Native names for it include *Jurema* and *Tepezcohuite*. Concoctions of the bark and leaves have been used to treat skin lesions, tooth pain and bronchitis. The wood is also used for fuel and the bark for tannin. The entheogenic connection is that the dried root bark of this plant has a DMT content of about 1%. This compares to a 0.68 % average DMT content in the *psychotria viridis* leaves, as mentioned above. The terms *jurema* or *vinho de jurema* refer to a psychoactive/entheogenic concoction made up of this root bark – which is combined with a second plant necessary to provide the MAO-inhibition. It's this combination of a DMT-containing and a MAO-inhibiting plant that causes it to be called, by some, an "ayahuasca analog."

In contemporary psychedelic underground circles the Mimosa

bark concoction is usually combined with the harmaline containing seeds of *Peganum harmala* – a plant not native to Brazil, but to Iran and Northwest India, where some speculate it may have been involved in the ancient Persian ceremonial drink *haoma*. Unlike the ayahuasca concoction, in which the DMT-containing *Psychotria viridis* leaves and the harmaline-containing *Banisteriopsis caapi* bark-pieces are brewed together for several hours, and then drank as one concoction, with Jurema the process has two steps. First, the ground-up and soaked harmala seeds are consumed up to one hour beforehand, de-activating the MAO-enzymes in the stomach; then the extract of *Mimosa hostilis* bark is drunk as a boiled or cold-water infusion. Effects are comparable to ayahuasca in terms of visions and body-sensations – but with less or no vomiting and nausea.

Jurema rituals in Brazil were thought to be extinct, until 1997, when a Brazilian woman named Yatra da Silveira Barbosa, having become familiar with the combination of ingredients necessary to produce the visionary concoction, traveled to Brazil to connect with the remote tribes still using the Jurema. Yatra had established a healing and addiction treatment center in Holland in the early 1990s, at first using ayahuasca in association with the *Santo Daime* church and then independently under the name *Friends of the Forest* and using the Jurema combination. When she traveled to Brazil in 1997, she found that the *caboclos* (ceremonial healers) were drinking the DMT-containing Jurema potion. But they had lost the knowledge of the admixture plant necessary to provide the MAO-inhibition – so their rituals had become "empty" ceremonies, and participants were not entering into visionary healing states.

In a beautiful example of ethnobotanical revitalization she

showed the tribal shamans how to use the non-native *Peganum har-mala* seeds which she had brought with her in combination with the Jurema concoction – and thus again restoring their capability to enter into visionary trance states. In an article in the MAPS Newsletter (1998) Yatra wrote that:

> "I brought awareness to the fact that when they drink Ju-rema (*Mimosa*) alone, the spirits (*encantados*) come to them in this material plane, and when they drink Jurema together with *Peganum*, the doors would open so that can visit the land of the enchanted themselves."

Psychedelics and neurotransmitters

Neurotransmitters are the chemicals identified in the human brain which account for the transmission of electrical signals from one neuron to another across synapses. The two most common neurotransmitters, accounting for excitatory or inhibitory action in 90% of the neurons in the brain, are GABA and glutamate. The major psychedelics interact primarily with the neurotransmit-ter serotonin, but also to varying degrees with norepinephrine, dopamine and acetylcholine. This has been known since the 1950s and is probably the reason for their "cross-tolerance" with each other. Cross-tolerance means that for a period of several hours after ingesting any one of the psychedelics, the individual will be "toler-ant," i.e. experience reduced or no effects, from a normal dose of any of the others.

In addition to their effects on serotonin release, the phenethyl-amines such as MDMA affect norepinephrine, which is the neu-rotransmitter mostly involved with the effects of stimulants such as amphetamine (also a phenethylamine). Perhaps this accounts for the more energizing, subjectively stimulating properties of the phenethylamines as compared to the tryptamines. On the level of subjective experience this can be observed if one compares the extremely rapid, almost percussive beat of the typical peyote chants, with the more sedate, mellow and melodic spirit healing songs sung by *ayahuasqueros* and mushroom *curanderas* like Maria Sabina.

Research in the last couple of decades has extended scientific understanding of the complexity and pervasiveness of serotonin in the human brain and nervous systems. Current research has localized the main effect of psilocybin and other tryptamine psychedelics at one receptor site specific from the dozen or more that are receptive for serotonin. Serotonin is called a "mood regulator," bringing both anger and depression back to a central balancing level. My own speculative hypothesis is that it is serotonin that is involved in the "expansion of consciousness," the heightening of awareness and understanding which can bring about a more balanced emotional attitude. Serotonin, in other words, may be the neurotransmitter for emotional intelligence or balance.

Neural circuits that use serotonin as their main neurotransmitter have been found in the *limbic-mammalian brain* systems that underlie much of our feeling life, especially the basic mammalian emotions (fear, rage, affiliation). Such neural circuits are also found in parts of the brain stem, called *reptilian brain* in Paul McLean's model. These findings are suggestively related to the sense of self-awareness, awareness of our evolutionary animal heritage, and the shamanic sense of connectedness or identification with animal consciousness.

Perhaps most provocatively, serotonin has been found to be the main neurotransmitter for the *enteric nervous system*, a system of 100 million neurons distributed in and around the intestinal tract.

This brain system is neuronically almost completely independent of the cerebral cortex. It is thought to be evolutionarily the oldest part of our nervous system. My speculation is that the role of serotonin in this brain system, and the possible effects of psychedelic drugs in it, may be the basis for experiences of evolutionary remembering, heightened instinctual or "gut-level" knowledge, and the healing of psychosomatic disturbances possible with psychedelics.

In addition to the action of tryptamines on serotonin receptors, there may be indirect effects of psilocybin on dopamine receptors as well. Some people think that dopamine is the neurotransmitter most involved in the experience of pleasure – for example, the "rush" of a cocaine high. The interaction with dopamine may account for some of the intense erotic-ecstatic sensations and feelings that can be part of the psilocybe mushroom effect.

Examination of the chemical structural formulae of the entheogenic and endogenous tryptamines reveals striking similarities and parallels, which are suggestive of systemic interactive effects, though they do not prove them. The basic core molecule, tryptamine, consists of an indole ring and an amine side chain. It is biosynthesized in the body from nutritional tryptophan, one of the essential amino acids. Serotonin is *5-hydroxy-tryptamine (5-HT)*, the tryptamine molecule with a hydroxy molecule in the 5-position. Serotonin itself cannot be absorbed via oral ingestion as it does not pass the blood-brain barrier. It is synthesized in the brain (probably in the pituitary and pineal glands) from tryptophan via the intermediate step of *5-hydroxy-tryptophan (5-HTP)*. Both tryptophan and 5HTP can be absorbed orally and act to increase serotonin levels in the brain; both have been and are used in the treatment of depression. Numerous studies link depression, as well anger, insomnia and addictive cravings, to serotonin deficiency which is treatable with 5-HTP. The well-known pharmaceutical creations known as the SSRIs (such as Prozac, Zoloft and others) also act to increase the amount of serotonin at the synapses, but they do this by selectively inhibiting the "re-uptake" of serotonin, thus preventing its storage, and making it more available at the synapse.

For further information on the role of different neurotransmitters in the human nervous system, the reader is referred to the chapter by J. C. Callaway in my edited anthology on ayahuasca; and the chapter by David Presti and David Nichols in my edited anthology on psilocybin mushrooms.

Selected psychoactive tryptamines

DMT - dimethyltryptamine

DMT and its derivatives, including 5-meo-DMT, cannot be absorbed when ingested orally, because they are broken down by MAO enzymes in the digestive system. In medical-pharmacological research, such as the research on DMT by Rick Strassman, MD, who called it the "spirit molecule," the drug is given by i.m. (intra-muscular) or i.v. (intra-venous) injection. In the informal underground culture, for obvious reasons, this method is rarely used, and the preferred method of ingestion is by smoking the free base, either from a water-pipe or sprinkled on a base of parsley, or by vaporizer inhalation.

The Shulgins and Trachsel, in their compendia on psychoactive tryptamines, give 60–100 mg as the dosage range for DMT, when smoked or inhaled, although Dale Pendell suspects (and I agree) this may be an error – the experiences they cite at the higher dose levels were largely dissociative. Jonathan Ott gives 25-30 mg as the (lower) threshold dose for smoked DMT.

My own estimates are that *25-30 mg is the ED-50 for smoked/inhaled DMT and 50-60 mg the DD-50*. The drug is extremely rapidly metabolized – the duration of effect after smoking inhalation is at most 5-10 minutes, barely enough to notice the swirling kaleidoscope of fractal patterns, with no discernible personal or cultural content. In *The Toad and the Jaguar* I cite a personal experience of both hellish and heavenly dimensions within less that 5 minutes of total elapsed time. With i.m. or i.v. administration, as in the studies by Strassman and some of our early experiments at Harvard, the effects are extended to about 45 – 60 minutes. (The injected dosages would also, of course, need to be considerably lower than with smoking). Because of the short duration of the DMT by smoking, and the impracticality of ingestion by snuffing because of the sheer quantity involved – I do not consider this substance by itself useful for purposes of entheogenic practice. I find it interesting too that my friend the late Terence McKenna, who became famous for his scintillating descriptions of DMT-inspired visions, more or less refrained from personal use in his later years.

Dale Pendell, in a chapter called *The Topology of the Between*, in his book *Pharmakognosis*, writes –

> DMT amplifies the mental perceptions of the eidetic imagery by so many orders of magnitude that the usual road signs of the ego, who I am, how I react to things, what kinds of things I say in such and such a situation, are lost. This flirtation with madness, with its accompanying twinge of terror, I think, in fairness, qualifies as a "thrill"(p. 234).

5-meo-DMT – 5-methoxy-dimethyltryptamine

Although much less known, both in research and underground circles, 5-meo-DMT is, to my mind, a much more interesting substance that may have far-reaching applications in medicine, pharmacology and psychotherapy. It is the subject of my monograph *The Toad and the Jaguar*, in which the "toad" refers to the Sonora Desert Toad, *Bufo alvarius*, which secretes 5-meo-DMT as part of its defensive venom; and "Jaguar" refers to a code name for this substance in underground circles, particularly when it is ingested intra-nasally, i.e. as a snuff. The use of plant preparations containing 5-meo-DMT as a snuff has been reported in several South American Indian tribes.

Both Shulgin and Trachsel give 6–20 mg as the "general dosage range" for 5-Meo-DMT ingestion by smoking or vapor inhalation. From the published data in the Shulgins' *TIHKAL* and on the internet, and from my own observations in underground research circles, I would estimate the *ED-50 of smoked or inhaled 5-Meo-DMT to be 5 mg and the DD-50 – 15 mg*. This means that 5-meo-DMT is approximately five to six times the potency of DMT – i.e. much less of the substance is needed to achieve the desired intensity of experience. This also has the consequence that it is relatively easy to ingest 5-meo-DMT by snuffing or smoking – an effective dosage is a small sliver of powder that can be insufflated or inhaled in one draw. On the other hand, smoking an effective dose of DMT (50-100 mg of the powder) requires usually at least three or four strong inhalations; and it would be painful and virtually impossible to ingest that amount of powder via nasal insufflation.

A further advantage of the snuffing method is in the duration of the effect: when smoked, 5-meo-DMT lasts about 10-15 minutes, slightly longer than the simpler molecule DMT; whereas when ingested as a snuff, it takes about 5-10 minutes for onset, and lasts 50-75 minutes – especially when ingested in a two-stage process, as described in *The Toad and The Jaguar*. In this process, after preparatory meditation, a 5 mg ED-50 threshold dose is snorted first – which will produce noticeable effects of muscular relaxation and sensory perception of smooth, warm fluidity in all parts of the body, as well as simple changing patterns of visual color. The peak effect occurs at about 20-30 minutes. It's sort of analogous to finding your "sea-legs" on a boat – your body recognizes and relaxes with the effect of the medicine. Many people can use this level of effect to explore current issues in their lives as well as psychosomatic healing. Those who desire to go to deeper levels, may then choose to ingest, via the nose, another 5-10 mg, which would facilitate a deepening and extension of the experience for another 50-60 minutes from the second point.

Other synthetic psychoactive tryptamines

Shulgin lists 55 items in his compendium *TIHKAL* ("Tryptamines I Have Known And Loved") for which he gives the chemical synthesis of each substance, as well as experience reports and ratings from his group of collaborators. Since the publication of his books in the early 1990s, more have been identified on internet websites like *Erowid* and some of their effects described by underground psychonauts (to use Jonathan Ott's term) – with varying degree of reliability. The following discussion of these psychoactive tryptamines describes some selected substances of which I have some personal knowledge and observations. I have particularly selected those which have a relatively brief time period of psychoactivity – since they are more likely to find applicability and usefulness in above-ground medical/psychiatric research. None of these synthetic psychoactive tryptamines have displaced psilocybe mushrooms in popular underground appeal. But they could be of interest to medico-psychiatric researchers and government health agencies who tend to prefer the precise dosage calibration possible with the synthetics.

DPT – dipropyltryptamine

In the early 1960s, this substance was used in a research program of psychedelic therapy with terminal cancer patients at Spring Grove Hospital in Baltimore,MD, conducted by William Richards, in collaboration with Walter Pahnke and Stanislav Grof. DPT is considered a sacrament by a New York based religious group known as the *Temple of the True Inner Light*. The sacrament in this group is referred to "The Angel of the Host" and is either smoked or drunk in their ceremonies. Remarkably, they have been unmolested by any government agency.

Shulgin gives *100-250 mg as the oral dosage range of DPT*, with a 2-4 hour duration. At dosages above 200 mg, there are uncomfortable sensation-feelings that are described as "exhausting." The psychedelic effects of DPT have been described as DMT-like and LSD–like, though the time course would make it much more useful in therapy applications than these better-known substances. In an article published on the *Erowid* website in 1998, the underground researcher known as *Toad* confirms the similarity of DPT with DMT and 5-meo-DMT, while emphasizing that there is enormous variability in physical and subjective effects and mentions a kundalini-like body vibration at excessive dosages. He suggests 20-100 mg is the range for smoking the freebase form – with effects lasting about 20 minutes; and 25-50 mg for snorting the Hcl salt, with effects lasting about 2 hours.

DET – diethyltryptamine

Shulgin and Trachsel both give *50-100 mg as the oral dose range*, with 2-4 hour duration. Both sources also report trials with DET either injected or smoked. Shulgin reports on a study done in the 1950s, where the drug was given in a clinical setting and the subjects, some of whom were neurotic and/or psychotic, were given a battery of psychological tests while on the drug; the results were predictably dysphoric. He also reports a different study where it was given to friends and associates of the researchers, in a relaxed supportive setting; the results were largely euphoric, thereby confirming once again the set-and-setting hypothesis. Trachsel mentions "contemplative and partly euphoric" effects, as well as synesthesia when listening to music, with DET. It's relatively short duration and minimal "body load" has much to recommend it as a possible adjunct to psychotherapy, especially at the lower dosages.

4-HO-DET – 4-hydroxy-diethyltryptamine

Shulgin and Trachsel both give *10-25 mg as the oral psychoactive dose range* of this substance – an advantage of potency over DET. But the estimated 4-6 hours for the duration of effect is a definite disadvantage compared to DET. The German psychiatrist Hans-Carl Leuner conducted studies of this substance (which he referred to as *CZ-74*) in the late 1950s and early 1960s, both in experimental and psychotherapeutic contexts. One of the most profound mystical experiences described in Shulgin's *TIHKAL*, "becoming immersed in the ground of Being, in Brahman, in God, in Ultimate Reality" occurred with 15 mg, orally, i.e. a relatively low dose. At

20mg and above, the experiences described were mostly described being dysphoric and having excessive "body load." These findings suggest that even lower dosages – less than 10 mg, could give good results as adjuncts to psychotherapy.

4-HO-DIPT – 4-hydroxy-diisopropyltryptamine.

Both Shulgin and Trachsel give *15-20 mg as the oral psychoactive dose*, and 2-3 hours as the duration of effect. The *Erowid* site gives 5-20 mg as the range from "threshold" to "common." Thus both potency and duration of effect make it a suitable support for psychotherapy. Shulgin reports that a 20 mg dose provided a "magical plus-four transcendental experience;" adding that "if there will ever be an acceptance of drugs such as these, in a psychotherapeutic context, a short duration is of extreme value to both the patient and the therapist." The termination of the effect was consistently described as almost "abrupt" – not a gradual decline. Some leg and body tremors were also reported by several subjects as the effects started.

4-Acetoxy-DIPT

This close chemical relative of the above, related the way psilocybin and psilocin are related, is not listed explicitly in Shulgin's *TIHKAL*, but on the *Erowid* website there is a compilation of reports by K. Trout, summarizing the experience of about 45 people with this substance, taken orally. *A standard dosage is listed as 15-30 mg,* with 40 mg producing physically unpleasant and emotionally dysphoric effects. Trout's summary description says the experience with this substance has a "gentle and benevolent nature…and seems to work in a non-threatening way…(producing) luscious sensual body feelings." Visual effects and changes are not particularly dramatic, but sexual intimacy can be enormously enhanced. His subjects report strong empathogenic qualities and suggests that it enhances "truthful communication and (could be) a potential agent for intensive self-analysis in psychotherapy."

5-MeO-DIPT

Both Shulgin and Trachsel give the *effective oral dosage range as being 5-12 mg* – thus its high potency requires careful measuring of dose; the duration of effect is 4-8 hours. Both authors cite reports of enhanced tactile sensation and consequently of aphrodisiac effects (dependent of course on set and setting) – leading to an internet nickname of "Foxymethoxy." On the negative side, some internet sources mention possible nausea and vomiting. Both Shulgin and Trachsel also mention some subjects experience "distortion" of sound and music perception. The *Erowid* website mentions nasal insufflation of this substance as a Hcl salt. At doses of *5-7 mg, this method of ingestion has the advantage of producing a trip lasting 1-3 hours*; higher doses prolong the effect. As such, it could have potential applications as an adjunct to psychotherapy and as support for meditation/divination. This substance has also reportedly been smoked, after conversion to free base: in this form the experience is even shorter, as with the other psychoactive tryptamines.

5-MeO-MIPT – 5-methoxy methylisopropyltryptamine

Shulgin gives *4-6 mg of this substance as an oral dose* and 4-6 hours duration; however only one of his subjects used this method of ingestion – all the others smoked it in doses of 12-20 mg, reporting that the effects most resembled 5-MeO-DMT, with episodes of dissociation and feeling-sensations of overwhelm at the higher dosages. Those dosages seem high compared to those reported on the *Erowid* website, which lists the oral dose range as 2-6 mg. Underground sources report use of *5-MeO-MIPT via insufflation, in the range of 3-5 mg* and with a duration of 1-2 hours. The effects of 5-MeO-MIPT via the snuffing method are essentially comparable to 5-meo-DMT, 5-MeO-DIPT and 4-Acetoxy-DIPT, as supports for meditation and spiritual practice; with 5-MeO-MIPT being the most potent – i.e having the lowest effective dosage threshold.

Selected psychoactive phenethylamines

MDMA – methylenedioxymethamphetamine

This drug, a creation of chemist Alexander "Sasha" Shulgin, first became known in the early 1980s in underground therapy circles under the code name *Adam*, where it was recognized as a remarkable non-hallucinogenic facilitator of empathic self-knowledge and interpersonal communication. I was one of a couple of dozen therapists who were initiated and trained in its use by Leo Zeff, whose history was later published in *The Secret Chief*, by Myron Stolaroff. I collected an anthology of experience reports with MDMA, some from my own files and some from other therapists, some in groups, some individual, and self-published them, with financial support from several friends, as *Through the Gateway of the Heart*, under the editorial *nom de plume* "Sophia Adamson."

The book came out in 1985, the exact year in which MDMA or "Ecstasy" as it had begun to be known in popular use, was put on the FDA's Schedule I list along with heroin, cocaine, marijuana and LSD – forcing all therapists who had been working with it, to either stop or go underground. The prohibition contributed to the spread of a global network of now criminalized recreational drug producers, who also collaborated with producers of mass light-sound-dance events known as "raves." The drug also was called just E or X in the underground culture and in it's latest incarnation is now apparently known and sold as "Molly." *Through the Gateway of the Heart* went out of print after 20 years, and has just been republished in a new edition – containing updated *Guidelines for the Sacramental Use of Empathogenic Substances.*

In German-speaking countries, MDMA and related non-hallucinogenic phenethylamines are referred to as "entactogens" – which means something like "touching within." In a minor academic difference among colleagues, I argued instead for the term "empathogen" – which means "empathy-generating," and this term has found some adherents as well among researchers. In my view the most significant psycho-pharmacological effect of MDMA, distinguishing it from all other hallucinogens and crucial in its function in the treatment of PTSD and other forms of anxiety, is the absence of fear and effortless movement into an empathic interpersonal position. I describe the applications of MDMA as an adjunct to psychotherapy in an essay titled *MDMA, Empathy and Ecstasy*, in a forthcoming volume in honor of Alexander Shulgin, its "re-discoverer."

Dale Pendell, in *Pharmako/Dynamis*, lists MDMA in its own group *Empathogenica* – sub-titled "mammalian raptures." Besides MDMA, this group of substances only contains Nutmeg (*myristica fragrans*) and *GHB*.

> The great opener of the heart chakra. Heart speech, heart words, spoken and listened to and heard and felt. Release of compassion. Touching. A mammalian thing, lying together in a pile like sea lions on a rock.

We had sex on the first date, X on the second. Then we got married. More marriages may have been broken by MDMA than saved. *Adam* makes it okay to say - I'm not happy.

If you are not in paradise, the E will show you. If you are in paradise, you already know.

A medicine for alienation. Which may account for its popularity (*op.cit.* pp. 216-220).

The Shulgins give the dosage range of MDMA as 80-150mg, and the length of the experience as 4-6 hours; Trachsel's figures are the same. From my own experience as a therapist in the early 1980s, I would estimate the *ED-50 to be somewhat lower, around 60-70 mg* – doses as low as that have been used by recipients of body-work or massage; and I agree that the *DD–50 is around 150 mg*. It should be noted that dosages at the medium level may be accompanied by repetitive, involuntary unconscious jaw movements and teeth-grinding. At the higher end of the dosage range, these kind of physical automatisms increase. As with other drugs in the amphetamine family, there is a distinct and even abrupt decline in physical and emotional responses after 3 ½ to 4 hours – which many people in the rave underground culture seek to counteract with repetitive dosing, sometimes three or four times a night. It goes without saying that such over-use can readily lead to a kind crash and a feeling of being drained – which is probably be due to the depletion of brain serotonin levels. Addictive over-use does seem to be a liability with MDMA, as with other phenethylamines.

With the phenethylamines like MDMA, 2-CB and others, higher dosages above the DD-50 given here don't actually lead to dissociation, because the individual may still be quite aware of current surroundings. What does occur is a kind of "body load" of hyperstimulation, elevated pulse, sweating, dysphoria, anxiety and a feeling of "wanting it to be over." Typically, one does not find the complex paranoid scenarios leading to dangerous actions, that are possible with dissociative dosages of the tryptamines and LSD. The individual just wants the experience to be over and the distressing body sensations eventually wear off; and this can be assisted by sleep medication.

2-CB – 4-bromo-2,5-dimethoxyphenethylamine

Although 2-CB is in the same chemical family as MDMA, it is somewhat different in that at the higher dosages, visual and even kinaesthetic sensory enhancement may occur. The Shulgins give a dose range of 12-24 mg, and a duration of 4-8 hours. Trachsel gives a dose range of 5-25 mg, and similar length of effect, though it should be mentioned the duration of effect is always dose-dependent. Both Shulgin and Trachsel mention visual and sensory enhancement, kaleidoscopic, three-dimensional, even holographic visuals at the higher dosages. Enhancement of erotic sensory and touch sensations are reported, including orgasm (dependent on set amd setting of course). There is an underground legend, its veracity unknown, that Sasha Shulgin, frustrated that his well-known creation MDMA seemed to inhibit orgasmic response, got inspired to tweak the molecule and came up with 2-CB, which then became his personal favorite. From my own surveys, I would concur with Trachsel that the *ED-50 of 2-CB is 5mg and the DD-50 is 25 mg* – although, as with the other dosage estimates, there is considerable individual variation in response intensity and length of effect.

According to an article published on the *Erowid* website, after Shulgin published his glowing account of the possible aphrodisiac effects of 2-CB, in the early 1990s, independent European pharmaceutical firms began marketing 2-CB, under the code name

Nexus in doses of 5 mg as treatment for impotence or frigidity. Of course this did not prevent underground users taking many times that dose and having profound psychedelic experiences – with or without the sex-enhancing qualities.

For longer recreational or personal growth oriented experiences, some circles take MDMA first, and then after the peak has passed in about 2-3 hours, take a dose of 2-CB, thereby extending the whole experience. The Shulgins say of the 2-CB effect: "It's as if the mental and emotional discoveries can be mobilized and something done about them" (*PIHKAL* p. 505).

On the internet website *Erowid*, one will also find advocates for the opposite sequence, who say that MDMA, taken 2 hours after the dose of 2-CB would tend to "soften" the extended stimulation of 2-CB. For unknown reasons, Shulgin's favorite 2-CB, which was still legal for some time after MDMA had already been scheduled, also entered the underground psychoactive drug scene in South Africa. Here this drug was apparently accepted by some of the traditional healers, called *sangomas*, as a valuable adjunct to their indigenous practices, particularly because dwelling in the townships they could no longer access their traditional plant medicines. In the Xhosa language this pharmaceutical was called *Ubalawu Nomathotholo*, which translates as "Medicine of the Singing Ancestors." Subsequently, it has also been placed on the prohibited substances list in all countries.

MDA – methylenedioxyamphetamine

This became known as the "love drug" during the late 1960s and early 1970s, and was used at dance parties called "raves." The Chilean psychiatrist Claudio Naranjo had worked with it and other psychoactive substances in his practice in the early 1960s and referred to MDA, in his book *The Healing Journey*, as the "drug of analysis." He stated that "regression occurs so frequently and spontaneously that it can be considered a typical effect of the substance". However, given the fact that Naranjo tested the substances only in a psychoanalytic setting and that MDAs more widespread usage was in dance parties – it seems more likely that the "analysis" was a "set and setting" effect. Both Shulgin and Trachsel give *80-150 mg as the dose range*, and the length as 8-12 hours. Once MDMA was discovered, in the 1980s, MDA gradually fell out of favor as a therapy adjunct, both because the speed-like stimulant component was stronger than with MDMA, and because of the longer duration of the effect.

MBDB – methylenedioxyphenylbutane

The general effect of this substance seems similar to MDMA in inducing a state of friendly equanimity ("even-heartedness") but with less emotional intensity. The lesser intensity of feeling, compared to MDMA, probably makes it less attractive as a party drug, and it is apparently not widely used in the rave dance underground. This difference is however potentially an advantage from the point of view of its use in psychotherapy. At the higher dosages of MDMA the positive affect generated by the substance may overwhelm any interest in psychological problem-solving. This is in fact precisely what happened to me, when I was working with it in the early days when MDMA (then known as *Adam*) had just become available as a therapeutic adjunct. A client of mine was literally unable to tune into any negative feelings she had towards her husband when the drug effect started – although she had chosen to work on this issue beforehand.

Shulgin and Trachsel both give 180-210 as the dosage range of MBDB and 4-6 hours as the duration of effect. The longer duration than MDMA, which correlates with dosage, would obviate any advantage as a psychotherapy adjunct, where shorter time-periods are advantages. But the Shulgins and Trachsel don't report any tests with lower doses and no boosters. Preliminary tests that I conducted with a group of 7 experienced subjects showed that at *dosages between 100-150 mg*, with no booster, *MBDB lasts 2 to 2.5* hours – which would make it a more useful psychotherapy adjunct from that point of view also.

Ketamine

In a completely different chemical family than the classical phenethylamines or tryptamines, ketamine is categorized as a "dissociative anesthetic," producing complete anesthesia at higher dosages and mostly abstract visual effects at lower dosages. Pharmacologically it appears to function as an antagonist at the NMDA-type glutamate receptors in the brain. In this respect it is like nitrous oxide, an anesthetic which attained notoriety and recreational usage in the late 19th century as "laughing gas." Ketamine also has been diverted to some extent into the recreational underground scene, although since it produces severe dissociation at the higher dosages – there is considerable danger associated with its use. I have been at "parties" in Europe, where ketamine was injected and people staggered around, more or less completely out of it, causing harm to themselves and others.

Ketamine is available by prescription in the US, for the treatment of chronic pain, although it's value in the treatment of pain is limited compared to synthetic opiates because of the shorter time duration of effect, typically 1 to 2 hours for a median dose. Trachsel gives the dosage range for i.m. injection as 30-120 mg; for nasal insufflation 50–150 mg; and as oral dose 200-450 mg. Recently, in the US at least, oral lozenges in 50 mg dosages have become available by prescription, for self-medication for chronic pain. At that dosage, people are still able to function normally, with the intensity of pain somewhat attenuated. I myself found this dosage level – 50-60 mg – very valuable when I was dealing with a bout of the *herpes zoster* virus in my facial nerves, where the low-dose ketamine ameliorated the otherwise constant excruciating pain, without putting me into an opiate-like haze.

From the point of view of the exploration of states of consciousness, the sub-anesthetic dosages are the most useful, yielding the most information for the self-study of consciousness transformations. Perception of one's body and one's surroundings seems to hover just slightly above and slightly below some kind of awareness threshold. I once participated as a subject in an experiment where an anesthesiologist had us connected to a continuous intravenous drip of ketamine, and had an associate ask us every 5 minutes "where are you now?" What he observed and concluded is that the subjects drifted off into a sleep-like twilight-state, from which we were awakened by the question – then struggled to verbalize what was happening, before drifting off again. This might be the reason that most people with ketamine describe the experience as pleasurable and dream-like, but are at a loss when pressed to describe details of what they are or were seeing or thinking.

I have also collaborated in group experiments where we decided to study the low-dose ketamine-state with the intention of staying fully awake and aware. Strong rhythmic music was played, that had been designed and recorded to help learning-disabled children stay task-focused. In addition, during the ketamine state, meditation instructions were given, and subjects reminded, every five minutes or so, to refocus attention on their perceptual and bodily responses, as well as noting any images or thought-forms drifting through their awareness. After about an hour, as the ketamine had worn off, a small amount of cannabis was smoked – one or two inhalations. Thus, the participants could compare three states of consciousness: the normal waking state, the ketamine state and the cannabis state.

The results were as one might expect: during the ketamine journey, participants lay completely still, reporting afterwards they were immersed in mostly abstract geometric shapes with pastel colors, very few human forms or faces, and in a peaceful mood without anxiety or excitement. When asked to touch their face or hands during this phase, they reported their skin felt as though it was some kind of fabric or paper – i.e. the anesthesia is first noticed in the sense of touch. In the cannabis phase of the experiment, the most dramatic change was the return of tactile sensation to almost erotic hypersensitivity.

Our group then performed a further experiment to see if the ketamine-induced state of emotional tranquility could be used therapeutically. Participants were asked, before the session, to choose one anxiety-laden episode or period from their past. Then, after taking the ketamine (an oral dose of 50 mg), and in that induced state of emotional tranquility, they were to evoke that situation again, when the usual emotional turmoil around that memory had been greatly attenuated or eliminated. This appeared to be a useful practice for working with past traumas. It was clear that it was important to have the intention and select the painful memory beforehand – because otherwise the neutralizing pleasantness of the ketamine state was likely to lead to forgetting the task.

The ketamine-induced explorations did not seem to be conducive of new insights or realizations. It was more like the healing of old wounds and traumas, whether physical or emotional, accompanied by a calm, detached but benevolent attitude.

Some have proposed that the ketamine-induced state is analogous to the near-death experience (NDE) sometimes reported by people who have survived a close encounter with physical death. There is a vast literature based on interviews with people who have survived close encounters with actual bodily death and returned to tell the tale. In my book *The Life Cycle of the Human Soul* I discuss the suggested comparison of NDE with psychedelic experiences. I concluded that while the sense of being completely detached from sensory awareness of one's physical body is common to both types of experience (especially with ketamine) "psychedelic experiences rarely, if ever, involve the features of classic near-death experience – such as looking down on one's body from above (OBE) or meeting deceased relatives and angelic escorts"(*op.cit.* p.72). The crucial distinguishing feature of NDEs from drug-induced "ego-death" experience seems to be the perception, at some level, that the heart has actually stopped.

Dale Pendell discusses ketamine in *Pharmakognosis*, under *Daimonica*, a classification that also includes the tropane alkaloids, CO_2, Amanita muscaria and iboga. His chapter on ketamine is called *The Art of Necromancy*. Necromancy is the art and practice of communicating with the spirits of the dead – and I must say in none of my own experiences with ketamine or those that I have witnessed, has anyone ever reported communicating with the dead, or thinking that they were dead.

A golden-yellow honeycomb, hexagons, suspended, stretching hundreds of thousands of feet below and above.

It started quickly enough. Easy and floating, but then things
began to slip and gain momentum. The acceleration was im-
pressive and it kept going. And then it was going too fast to
hang on, but it didn't stop. And then I saw the world behind
this world.

I call it the Yellow World because that was the predominant
color of the world. There were abstract equivalents of wheels
and cogs and levers. It was something like the machinery of
the universe and though it was extremely intricate it wasn't
static or delicate and huge fluid-like drops would explode
out of nothing. The inner structure of self-spaces. It's abstract and colorful but it's yours (Pendell, D. *op.cit.* pp. 273-
280).

Many years ago, when I first started experimenting with ketamine, I was making the assumption that being a lab-manufactured
drug, rather than a plant or fungal preparation with shamanic pedi-
gree, one would not see or sense "spirits" under the influence of this
substance. This proved to be wrong. In one ketamine experience
I had, when we injected about a 100 mg while listening to some
angelic harp music, I suddenly "saw" a flight of rose-colored flying
spirits, who were sweeping down over the earth and actually into
the earth, through the rocks and soil and then back up and out – all
the while singing ecstatically, something like "we love the Earth, we
love the Earth." Needless to say, I was impressed. I realized once
again that the visions that one sees cannot really be said to be a
function or a product of the drug. We should say instead that our
perception of subtler dimensions of reality can at times be triggered
by this and other substances, facilitated always by the factors o set
and setting – in this case the hearing of the angelic harp-music.

Salvia divinorum – "Sage of the Diviners"

This herb of the mint family, used by the Mazatec Indians of Mexico for divination is referred to also as *Ska Maria Pastora, Yerba de María* or *Hojas de la Pastora*. References to a "shepherdess" are strange, since the Mazatecs don't have sheep. The hallucinogenic properties of this plant, its mythic ancestry in the pre-Christian cultures of Mexico and its contemporary use in divination, were brought to the attention of Western science in the early 1960s by R. Gordon Wasson and Albert Hofmann, who had previously been instrumental in bringing the visionary psilocybe mushrooms to the attention of the modern world. Their curandera informant, the legendary Maria Sabina, told Wasson and Hofmann, that they used the *Salvia divinorum* for their divinations when weather conditions made the visionary mushrooms unavailable.

Although Hofmann and Wasson reported on *Salvia divinorum* and its use in divination in the 1960s, it only became more widely known and used in underground circles in the 1990s, when people started preparing and smoking the fortified leaves. The phytochemistry of *Salvia divinorum* is unique: the psychoactive principle has been identified as *Salvinorin A*, a diterpenoid, unlike all other psychedelic substances which are chemically alkaloids. *Salvinorin A* as a purified extract is extremely potent, i.e. psychoactive in humans in doses of 250 micrograms, exceeded in potency only by LSD. Because of the extreme potency there are real dangers of a toxic psychosis from careless ingestion of the purified substance. Summarizing the known pharmacology, Daniel Siebert states that *salvinorin A* is a selective kappa opiod receptor agonist: through self-experiments he confirmed that the effects of *salvinorin A* are inhibited by pre-administration of the opioid receptor agonist, naloxone. There are several different kinds of opioid receptor agonists – and those activated by *Salvia divinorum* are quite different than those activated by the opiates like morphine. Thus, Salvia does not reduce pain, in fact enhances sensitivity and is not addictive.

The traditional Mazatec way of ingesting the diviners sage was to roll the fresh green leaves into a thick cigar-like wad and keep it stuffed in your mouth next to the gums, where it is slowly absorbed through the mucous membranes over a period of ten to twenty minutes. Most Westerners have found this process too laborious. Combined with the extreme bitter taste and limited accessibility to fresh leaves, this method of ingestion is rarely used in contemporary contexts. However Dale Pendell, in his encyclopedic treatises on mind-assisting plants and fungi, gives detailed information on this traditional method of ingestion and its benefits, as does Daniel Siebert, who is perhaps the leading exponent of the values and virtues of this particular plant. The traditional method or something like it, is probably the safest, because of the tricky and unpredictable nature of individual reactions to smoking enhanced Salvia leaf preparations and even more so the purified *salvinorin-A*.

Contemporary explorers may smoke the dried leaves of the plant, which produces a mild, transient "high" generally not as colorful as smoked cannabis by itself – though it may offer a distinctive addition to a smoking mixture containing cannabis and other herbs such as damiana leaf, as well as natural tobacco.

More commonly, an alcohol extract from the Salvia leaves is made, applied to a batch of the leaves and these *enhanced* or *fortified* leaves are then smoked. The potency of the extract will vary considerably because of natural variations in the potency of the crude leaf. An extract from 5 grams of dried leaves applied to 1 gram of leaves is then referred to as 5x. There are several websites that offer these enhanced leaves for sale – at potencies from 5x to

20x, 40x and even 100x. The experience resulting from one or two inhalations of the smoking mixture (which must be held in the lungs for better absorption) will generally last for 5-10 minutes, but can be extended by repeated inhalations. In this form the smoked Salvia can leave a mellow after-glow that can last for several hours. There are several websites with instructions for growing the plant as well as websites that offer instructions for preparing the extracts. Because of the different concentrations of the extracts in these preparations, it is virtually impossible to give general guidelines for dosages. Those wishing to use these plant preparations for entheogenic explorations, need to prepare themselves by becoming thoroughly informed – and preferably growing and making their own medicine plant allies.

The 2013 book by Ross Heaven – *Shamanic Quest for the Spirit of Salvia* – offers a number of accounts from about fifty friends and associates with the smoking of the different enhanced leaf preparations. Like some other writers on *Salvia divinorum*, Ross Heaven seems impressed by the apparent uniqueness of the Salvia experience compared to other entheogens. In his book, he lists the following as common themes of the reported experiences with Salvia – augury (foretelling), questioning one's sense of self, fascination with the symbolic meaning of borders and edges, sense of other dimensions and universes, remembering or re-experiencing childhood scenes, experiencing other time periods not personally remembered, sensations of different types of movement and wheels of various kinds, telepathy and empathy with others, zen-like paradoxicality, themes of love and karma and a perceptual focus on membranes and two-dimensional surfaces.

All these themes, *except for the occasional perceptual focus on flatness and two-dimensionality*, have been noted as common effects of all psychedelic drugs, including LSD, psilocybin, ayahuasca, mushrooms, DMT and others. The disruption of three-dimensional perception and reduction to "flat-land" awareness may be unique to this substance. Indeed the classic psychedelics usually lead to an enhanced depth perception, if eyes are open and looking at the natural environment.

One may speculate about the symbolic meaning of this flattened perceptual field, and the informants in Heaven's book do manage to extract some personal meaning from their Salvia visions, flatness and all – especially if they had formulated some personal intentions beforehand. However, the anomalous perception may simply be an indication that the brain circuits involved in depth perception are being selectively affected. This would be a worthwhile area of psychopharmacological research. It may also be a dosage effect, which only appears after ingestion of the higher concentration dosages.

My own experiences, which have mainly been with the lower dosages, has not included any of these "flat-land" visions – nor have I so far heard of any useful divinatory knowledge or insight resulting from such perceptions. Another possible confounding factor in understanding these two-dimensional, flattening effects – is the fact that traditionally, the Salvia leaves are held in the mouth and their essence absorbed over a considerable period of time, while the voyager is in more or less total darkness. The smoking method of several deep inhalations obviously requires the eyes to be open as the effects are starting – and two-dimensional brain images are perhaps being projected and mixed with external perceptions. Keeping the eyes closed during the journey would avoid such dimensional confusions.

In comparing the plant-spirit of *Salvia divinorum* with that of cannabis, I have heard it said that the spirit of Salvia is like a shy girl who stays in the background until she knows you – as the plant grows best in shaded locations out of direct sun. On the other hand, the spirit of cannabis is like the laughing girl with a red dress on – as the cannabis herb likes direct sunlight. People laugh a lot smoking cannabis – not so much with Salvia.

Dale Pendell, in *Pharmacopoeia*, has *Salvia divinorum* in the category *Existentia*, a unique category with only one member. Here are some of the things he writes about Salvia:

> Some say it is a sensual and a tactile thing. Some say it's about temporality and dimensionality…or about becoming a plant.

> The effects are different, depending on how the plant is ingested, on whether you meet the ally on the Path of Leaves or by crossing the Bridge of Smoke. And also depending on whether the plant has accepted you. That's metaphorical. Or is it?

> To visit the *hojas de la Pastora* is to visit an oracle, and she should be approached with the same reverence. It lights up the souls of those around us: we hear/know what they really think, what they really want, what they really want to have done. It's ideal for couples work, for keeping in touch.

> Vowel sounds change the colors; pitch and tone alter the shape of the enclosing space; semantics create texture. Sentences become palpable things, they take visible and tactile forms, flying or sinking. But all in the mind's eye, not in the eye-ball.

> It just gives you where you are. Wherever you are, that is what you get. If you are in darkness, you fly through darkness. The light and faces you see are the faces you always carry, the mental faces, lit by the glow of the mind. If you are with your lover, the plant is an aphrodisiac (Pendell, D. *op. cit.* pp. 156-176).

Daniel Siebert is a writer-explorer who has done an enormous amount of careful research on Salvia, published on his web-site (www.sagewisdom.org), prior to publication of a book-in-progress. This website is a treasure trove of information, as well as a source for obtaining plant and elixir preparations. He has pointed out that besides the smoking of crude and enhanced leaf preparations, there is a further method of ingesting Salvia that is closest to the traditional Mazatec method of chewing the fresh leaves: this method involves ingesting an alcohol extract of *Salvia divinorum* and letting it absorb slowly through the mucous membranes of the mouth. This method, which can involve one or several droppers of the alcoholic tincture – allows for a carefully calibrated ingestion and produces an experience that can last for 30 to 40 minutes, and thus allows for more extended divinations than is possible with the smoking method. These extracts, which Siebert refers to as *Sage Goddess Emerald Essences* can be obtained from his website.

Siebert's website provides detailed information and guidance on the productive and safe usages of *Salvia divinorum* in its various forms. He has developed a 6-point intensity rating scale of Salvia experiences. Levels 1 and 2 involve subtle effects of altered visual and auditory perception and enhancement of aesthetic and sensual pleasure. Level 3 is a state with closed eye fractal and geometric visuals, though they dissipate with eyes opened. Level 4 involves complex visions and voices in which one becomes completely absorbed as long as eyes are closed. One tends to lose awareness of consensual reality and take the inner scenes for real. Levels 5 experiences involve disconnect from any sense of separate individuality – i.e. people may experience merging consciousness with God, or with a wall. Level 6 experiences are basically complete dissociated unconsciousness, in which the person's body may still be trying to move around and can harm themselves if not protected. Siebert mentions the "flattening" perception as a possible effect at Level 2 – but also the enhancement of depth perception.

From the point of view of doing interesting and therapeutically valuable divination work, the method of ingestion by taking the purified essence and letting it be absorbed through the mucous membranes of the mouth would seem to be by far the most useful. It leads to longer experiences – 30 to 40 minutes – plus after-glow; and it is closest to the traditional Mazatec method of letting the fresh leaves be slowly absorbed through the mucous membranes of the mouth. Also from the point of view of usefulness for thera-peutic divination the lower dosages or potencies would seem to be more valuable. Several of the people who in Ross Heaven's group who were therapists themselves, stated that while they learned something from their personal experiences at the higher potencies, they would not recommend using them to with patients or clients as part of their work.

In some of my own explorations with this substance I con-firmed again the value and importance of explicitly having a clear intention, ideally a diagnostic or healing intention, when working with this medicine ally. Trials where people say they "just want to see what it does" tend to lead to uninteresting findings at the lower doses and scary dissociative effects at higher doses. Or they might find themselves, as happened to me once, remembering or reliving an unhealed situation from their own life, that the Salvia spirit had somehow unerringly identified and presented to them – an experi-ence that can be as unnerving as getting an unexpected diagnosis of an unhealed disease process.

What is the real point or value of the flattening or loss of per-ceptual depth? It would seem that for valid diagnostic seeing one would want to "see into" the inner structure of whatever we are regarding. Is the flattening effect a teaching about the superficiality of our ordinary conditioned perception? I appreciated Daniel Siebert's response to a question on his website about whether Salvia is an entheogen? He wrote:

> More properly entheogen refers to a type of drug usage, not a type of drug. Salvia CAN be used as an entheogen. It is used as such when taken as part of a serious spiritual quest; but most 'Western' Salvia usage would not qualify as entheogenic.

In a couple of experiences I had with Salvia (smoking an enhanced mixture of 4x) some years ago, I was given some hints how the plant essence might assist in healing diagnosis – though I saw it would require training and practice of concentration. On one occasion, after inhaling the smoke I felt immobilized in a vividly articulated space, in which my body was somehow parked 'down there' and my mind awareness spread out throughout the room, and even the house. I began to think divining might work this way – you would be able to send your awareness into someone else's space – providing you could concentrate with intention. On another occasion, a friend and I smoked the enhanced leaf preparation, began to sense the "is-ness," the "just there" existential presence of things. I mentioned this briefly to my friend and then when I closed my eyes again, a really interesting thing happened. I felt as though my skull was a bowl that had been flattened open, leaving my brain exposed to pure perception of the environment, a "spreading out" kind of awareness.

Reflecting on these experiences, I realized I was experiencing the perception of a plant, or rather my usual human head had become the "head" or top of a plant. Then I took another hit of the smoke to see if I could confirm this by extending the plant awareness all throughout my body, not just the head. Sure enough – "I" turned into a leafy green plant, much like sage. Looking down (eyes closed of course) my trunk was a green stalk, all my inner organs were like the leaves, sort of "hanging out" from the central stalk, and all had turned into sense organs, sensing the environment – light, heat, chemicals, etc.

I realized that the fact that the sense perceptions of a plant are not buffered by skin, as in all of us animals, means that plant perception of the environment is enormously more sensitive than that of animals. The existential is-ness or rootedness I had felt before was the rootedness of a plant. The inner organs of my human animal body – liver, heart, stomach, etc – are all attached to the mesenteric trunk, just like the different leaves of a plant are all attached to the main trunk. As a plant, "I" would be completely exposed to the elements, or predatory attack. No escape was possible – but I didn't feel afraid or vulnerable – those typical mammalian emotions. It was just the "is-ness" of a plant's life. In any case, having your head cut off is not a big deal for a plant, as it would be for an animal – as a plant you would just grow another one.

From such experiences I began to realize how an experienced healer using the Salvia medicine might be able to move with sensing awareness into the body of another human animal, and perceive which organs are in failing health and what kind of energetic or nutrient support they might need – just like a gardener would tune into the needs of plants in his or her care.

I also began to understand the mythic story of the *Green Knight* in a new way. As I had written in my book *Green Psychology*, in the cycle of legends around King Arthur, the Green Knight (with green face, green armor, green helmet, green helmet, and mounted on a green horse) arrives one day at the royal court and issues a challenge to any of the knights present: he will submit to having his head cut off, and the knight who does so must then surrender to decapitation one year later. After considerable hesitation, Sir Gawain accepts the challenge and cuts off the head of the Green Knight. The Green Knight then calmly picks up his head, tucks it under his arm, and rides away, promising to meet Gawain in a year's time, to fulfill the vow. The rest of the story deals with the tests of his loyalty and integrity that Gawain has to undergo on his way to meet the Green Knight. Thus, the Green Knight is symbolically a personification of the regenerative power of the plant realm, to which the proud human being must submit or pay the price.

Cannabis sativa and Cannabis indica

The hemp plant has a rich and ancient history in Eastern and Western cultures as a healing remedy and a stimulant of creative visions. It has also been a focal issue for many of the culture wars of the 20th century – leading to tens of thousands of lives lost to imprisonment for victim-less crimes. These culture wars in the West may now be entering a new phase, as increasing numbers of US states and other countries are moving toward decriminalization of recreational use and advancing research on its multiple healing potentials. On a related front, the socio-cultural struggles also involve efforts to re-introduce hemp farming into American agriculture – where, up until the early 20th century hemp had been a major source of fiber for rope, sails, clothing and building material, and hemp seed oil for paints and varnish, lamp lighting, nutrition and medicine.

A recent newsletter of the *Drug Policy Alliance*, a group that supports rational harm-reduction policies for all drug use, summarizes the current confirmed knowledge about the health effects of cannabis: (1) Marijuana smokers can have similar respiratory problems as tobacco smokers, but studies have shown that even regular and heavy use does not lead to lung cancer. (2) Smoking marijuana can rarely and temporarily raise the risk of myocardial infarction. (3) Meta-analysis failed to reveal a systematic effect on neuro-cognitive function in long-term regular users. (4) Studies of cannabis use in depression suggest that moderate use can have anti-depressant effects, but heavy doses can exacerbate depression. Marijuana does not cause schizophrenia, but may precipitate psychotic reactions in younger people predisposed toward them. (5) While some marijuana users can become addicted to the drug, the risk of dependency and the severity and social costs of addiction are significantly less than with alcohol and tobacco. (6) Marijuana is not a "gateway drug:" people who use other mind-altering and addictive drugs are likely to have also used cannabis, but most marijuana users never use any other illegal drug.

The range of documented health effects of cannabis is enormous and growing. It includes arthritis, asthma, chronic pain, depression, epilepsy, glaucoma, some tumors, insomnia, menstrual cramps, migraines, movement disorders, eating disorders, multiple sclerosis, nausea, appetite loss, skin conditions and others. In fact, its versatility in healing diverse conditions adversely affects the political prospects of cannabis being adopted into the system of "big medicine/big pharma," which prefers specific patentable remedies for specific conditions. A comprehensive summation of the social, medical, recreational and scientific aspects of marijuana has been recently published in the book *Smoke Signals*, by Martin A. Lee (2012).

Israeli scientist Raphael Mechoulam identified *THC (tetrahydrocannabinol)* as the chief psychoactive and medicinal ingredient in the cannabis plant. Significantly, Mechoulam and others have found that the bodies of human and all vertebrate animals contain an ancient *endocannabinoid* system inherent in several body organs. This functions as a part of an ancient endogenous immune system, allowing communication and coordination between different cell types.

Mechoulam has summarized the actions of this *endocannabinoid* system, which is stimulated and strengthened by ingested cannabis as follows: *relaxing* and thereby promoting rest and sleep; *stimulating appetite* and thereby countering nausea and wasting syndrome; *forgetting* and thereby alleviating the impact of daily stress. Mechoulam pointed out that while "forgetting" is normally thought of as a deficit, it is a definite plus in allowing us to forget the inevitable stresses of daily life and work. The memory impairment implies that you should avoid cannabis consumption when engaging in complex skills involving memory functions. Cannabis-induced memory deficit also probably underlies the oft-noticed reduction of dream recall, when cannabis is ingested before sleep. I have heard heavy regular pot users state that dream recall rebounded enormously when they discontinued smoking.

I would add four additional qualities of the cannabis experience, and presumably the *endocannabinoid* system: (1) heightened taste sense, which adds to the appetite stimulant effect; (2) enhanced touch sensitivity, which connects with the widely appreciated erotic stimulation; and (3) heightened auditory perception, traditionally known and appreciated by jazz musicians and music lovers of all kinds. This auditory effect may be an expression of a more basic time dilation effect which allows the "stoned" listener to appreciate a musical phrase in a kind of time-less auditory space.

A fourth oft-noticed cannabis effect are the spontaneous eruptions of irrepressible laughter without an obviously humorous stimulus situation. In the 2010 documentary film *What if cannabis Cured Cancer?* some of the subjects being interviewed while stoned in the research lab can barely contain their fits of laughter. However, the healing and immune-system strengthening effect of humor is well-known and expressed in the traditional motto that "laughter is the best medicine."

In an old R. Crumb cartoon that appeared sometime in the 1960s, the humor is linked to the time dilation: two very stoned-looking dudes are sitting on a porch in a small Western town, and a motorcyclist who has evidently just roared through town, is on the way out. One of the dudes turns to the other and says – "Man, I thought he'd never leave."

Dale Pendell, in *Pharmacopoeia*, classifies *Cannabis sativa* as the unique member of his group *Evaesthetica* – "sensually pleasing."

> Euphoria. Thought manifestation all the way to thought animation; formal structures seen on their own terms; aesthetic experiences, personal and sexual, all brought into high relief.
>
> More humor and wit, attention to ideas and innuendo, in the conversation. Or if not, at least rapt attention while you listen.
>
> Perhaps most astonishingly, hashish even seems to be able to assist in reading books in languages that one hardly knows; meaning floats up from hidden roots and cognates.
>
> Patterns emerge: visual patterns, larger structures and conversations in music, insights into others, and insights into self. Sensory enhancement: new tastes, new sounds, colors with a spiritual glow. High weirdness (*op.cit.* pp. 179-207).

Three

Precautions and Safety Factors

The art of healing is long and life is short,
the opportunity fleeting, the experiment dangerous,
the judgment difficult.

~Hippocrates, 'The Father of Medicine'

The issue of agreements or "rules" in group sessions with psychedelic substances elicits more diverse opinions and points of view than any other. The issue is moot for individual explorers, such as many of those reporting their research on internet web-sites. The issue is also moot in sessions conducted by a leader or guide, whose practices are explicitly or implicitly accepted by those who respond to the invitation to participate in a ritual. In self-organizing groups of peers, these issues are more likely to be explicitly discussed.

However, issues of safety and possible harm to self or others in the context of entheogenic ritual use need to be taken into account by responsible explorers, regardless of whether the group has a leader or is a group of experienced friends. This is in fact one of the main dividing criteria separating recreational use of psychedelic from their use for purposes of spiritual exploration, healing and creativity.

Confidentiality

An agreement about maintaining confidentiality as to the use of mind-expanding substances – almost all of which are illegal to possess in almost all contemporary nation states – is an essential prerequisite for engaging in the underground use of these substances. The only exception would be for participants in a DEA/FDA-approved medical research project, where the supply of technically "contraband" material is tightly controlled and supervised.

The primary reason for this agreement is of course the real danger of arrest and imprisonment for possession of contraband materials, or being in a place where contraband material is being consumed. For this reason the agreement should apply not only to the identities of the leader and all the persons participating in the session, but also to the center or residence and its owners where the event is taking place. This is not a prohibition against people sharing their experience with their loved ones or indeed anyone: they can relate their experience with the medicines to others as much as they want – they are just enjoined from mentioning names.

If one member of a married or living-together couple attends an entheogenic session without their partner, the individual will sometimes say (or think to themselves) "I share everything with my spouse or partner, because that is part of our intimacy commitment." In such situations it is important to realize that the confidentiality agreement covers the *names* of participants including the group leader, the place or location of the group ceremony (the exposure of which could have serious legal consequences) and the experiences that other people share in confidence. People can, of course, share the nature and details of their own personal experience with their partners, which could indeed be the welcome subject of intimate conversations and reflections.

This agreement becomes particularly relevant if one member of a couple is attending and the couple is in conflict, the partner is estranged or is opposed to or afraid of entheogen use, for whatever reason. It can then happen, as it did to a couple of my acquaintance in a European country, that a divorced but still embittered partner of one of the participants in a ceremony, informed the authorities that a session with illegal substances was taking place – leading to the arrest and imprisonment of the physician guiding the sessions. It is of course a moot question whether such a confidentiality agreement would have prevented this unfortunate turn of events – nor is it clear that such an agreement can always be obtained when spouses are battling. But at least the question deserves to be considered and discussed in advance in situations like that.

Another kind of situation can occur if a person attends or intends to attend a group or individual psychedelic session with psychotherapeutic healing intentions – and this person is in fact under a prescribing physician's care for some condition that involves psychotropic medication. There are several potentially tricky issues here: one is the use of other medications that might potentially interfere with or amplify or complicate the mind-expanding effect of the entheogens. The other issue arises if the primary care physician or treating psychiatrist is opposed to the use of psychoactive substances, or ignorant of their effects, or interaction effects. One resolution of this question, if it arises, is for the participant to obtain permission from their doctor and/or their psychotherapist to participate in a psychedelic session – while not disclosing the identity of the entheogenic guide (for reasons of confidentiality).

Public and professional knowledge of the therapeutic potentials of psychedelic substances is now so widespread, at least in the US or at least in California, that situations such as the following can easily arise: an underground psychedelic psychotherapist receives a request for a guided therapeutic session with MDMA for an individual with mixed diagnosis, accompanied by written letters from the individual's psychologist and consulting MD, requesting that particular form of treatment and offering their assurance of treatment follow-ups and back-up medication if needed. The treating professionals could not offer that treatment themselves, but could recommend it and refer the client to an "underground" therapist. More commonly perhaps, people resort to healing methods with psychedelics when they are no longer in medically supervised professional care, and are taking complete responsibility for their own well-being and use of medications.

There is a second reason for the explicit confidentiality agreement, and in some respects this is probably the more important reason. In groups with a circle or council structure in which people may share intimate details of their inner journey and family situation, the agreement that whatever is being revealed is totally confidential and not shared outside the circle is the essential trust-supporting factor that allows the teller of the story to reach into the deepest part of themselves for their sharing, and to feel and be safe in so doing. It is part of the ethic of such group council formats that there is never any implicit or explicit demand for anyone to share anything that they are not ready or willing to share.

The issue of recording in actual ceremonies and in the follow-up integration sessions also needs to be explicitly addressed. Different groups make different kinds of agreements. Surreptitious recording tends to create an atmosphere of suspicion and even paranoia – and reduces trust. In the groups that I've been connected with, there is no note-taking or recording either during the ceremony itself or when someone is reporting on their experience during the integration phase – to allay even the appearance of secret recording. These are some of the essential differences between a sacred ceremony as compared to a workshop or learning environment, where note-taking is encouraged. The speaker speaks from the Heart and from Spirit and the listeners listen with full attention from the heart-mind. The empathic and non-judgmental attention of the listeners acts as if magnetically to draw the speaker's story through to expression from the soul-core.

Pre-existing conditions and contra-indications

For individual psychotherapeutic treatment sessions held in a medical research clinic or addiction center – there is often a list of pre-existing conditions, which would lead those conducting the therapy or research sessions to exclude them. For example, the brochure for an ibogaine addiction treatment center in Mexico, lists among the medical contra-indications for treatment: active infections like pneumonia, AIDS/HIV, peptic ulcers, vascular disease, cancer (not in remission), brain disease, high blood pressure, bowel disease, kidney disease and others.

In self-directed, non-medical research and exploration groups like those using Shulgin's research protocol and others, there are usually no fixed rules about excluding someone because of pre-existing illnesses – although people who are not well at the time of the session may excuse themselves from participating. The participants in the session are not there to test some new treatment protocol for a medical condition, but for the exploration of varieties of states of consciousness. The traditional ceremonies with ayahuasca with mestizo guides are also not focused on curing any illness or overcoming any addictions. Western medical or psychiatric diagnoses or categories are not in their worldview, although some Westerners participating in traditional Amazonian ayahuasca ceremonies have indeed reported alleviation or even sometimes cures of long-standing chronic diseases, like cancer. The indigenous and *mestizo* shamans are more likely to see the purpose of the healing process to be the ridding of "bad spirits" that have somehow infested or infected the person – possibly by intentional sorcery.

The self-organizing hybrid shamanic-therapeutic groups that have arisen in Europe and North America during the past thirty years or so have usually or mostly adopted a practice of expecting or requiring participants not to be taking other mind-altering psychiatric medications, because of the possibility of unknown interactive effects between different drugs. It is widely understood that in the case of plant or fungal medicines that have been used by indigenous shamans for hundreds or perhaps thousands of years, the principle of natural selection will have ensured that the medicines as used by the native shamans are safe and contribute to a healthy and spiritually-centered way of life.

The same can emphatically not be said of new drugs produced in Western research laboratories – whether as officially approved drugs for certain medical or psychiatric conditions, or whether produced by underground chemists under conditions with varying levels of purity or toxicity. In addition, as Shulgin and other chemists and pharmacologists in this work have repeatedly emphasized, one cannot generalize from a few dozen trials in safe dose ranges to safety when taken repeatedly or in larger doses or in samples of unknown purity, as we know is the case for drugs like MDMA and its popular descendants or variants such as "ecstasy" or "molly."

In the case of ayahuasca, which is a combination of the tryptamine-containing plant *psychotria viridis*, and harmine/harmaline – containing vine *banisteriopsis caapi*, there is a specific toxic condition that can result in those who are taking medically prescribed SSRIs (selective serotonin re-uptake inhibitors) as anti-depressants and then taking ayahuasca, which increases brain levels of serotonin by blocking its metabolic breakdown. There is the possibility of a rare, but potentially dangerous toxic condition known as the "serotonin syndrome," caused by excessive levels of serotonin in the brain, that can result from the taking of ayahuasca together with pharmaceutical SSRIs. For details on this condition readers may consult the chapters by neurochemist J. C. Callaway and by myself in the book *Ayahuasca – Sacred Vine of Spirits*. Ayahuasca – itself a concoction of two separate plants – is not toxic in its cooked plant form and indeed has been proven to have a range of health-and wellness-supporting effects.

In the case of MDMA, the human pharmacology and safety issues have been intensively studied and documented for the purpose of FDA-approved research applications. The research literature reviews can be accessed by the general public on the website of the MAPS organization, which is one of the primary organizations conducting this research. As for *Ecstasy* in its popularized form, it has been distributed and consumed at dance and "rave" events in all parts of the world over the past twenty years, attended by hundreds of thousands (some estimate millions) of people, and the data collection has of necessity been unsystematic and sporadic.

While there have been some documented cases of overdose deaths, it is hard to come by hard data on the extent to which the drug consumed was pure MDMA, or a mixture with other drugs of unknown purity. Considering the huge numbers of participants in these events, the number of reported cases of adverse drug reactions is miniscule. In the first few years after the use of *Ecstasy* became popular at dance events, there were some deaths due to dehydration – hyperstimulated raving dancers were not aware of the need for frequent re-hydration and greedy event organizers were charging for bottled water. After some time, this factor became known and it has become part of the accepted social ethic of these events that plenty of water is always freely available, and there are spaces for people to "chill out" from the dancing and just relax and socialize.

Although the need for regular rehydration when MDMA or *Ecstasy* is taken (especially at large scale dance events) is recognized, there is a lesser known and rarer physiological danger that can arise with MDMA – when water is consumed excessively leading to *hyponatremia*, or "water intoxication." The excessive water consumption disturbs the balance of sodium and potassium electrolytes, which disrupts the functions of the nervous system – which, if not checked, can lead to diarrhea, over-salivation, stupor, vomiting, muscle tremors, confusion, frequent urination, and potentially fatal brain damage. Drinking sport drinks, rather than just pure water, will keep salt and electrolyte levels balanced and can prevent *hyponatremia*. Coconut juice, which contains a healthy balance of the necessary minerals and electrolytes, is a useful alternative to pure water, but any balanced electrolyte drink will help prevent both overheating (*hyperthermia*) and water poisoning (*hyponatremia*).

In this book, I am not describing or discussing the issues of drug safety precautions and adverse reactions at mass events like raves or Burning Man. The *MAPS* organization and groups such as *Dancesafe*, have developed their own safety and training protocols for such events. In this book we are concerned with small-scale group and individual experiences dedicated to healing, exploration and psychospiritual growth. In these smaller groups focused on intensive and psychotherapeutic inner work and not involving vigorous physical activity, issues such as the serotonin-syndrome or hyponatremia are unlikely to arise.

Exceptions to this generalization my however occur if there is a pre-existing medical condition – which may be unknown to the individual, or known but denied and concealed by the individual. An example of the unknown existence of a pre-existing contra-indication occurred to a Swiss psychiatrist who was working in France with a group of people, using ibogaine therapy. One of the participants had an undiagnosed and undisclosed heart condition and died during the session. The psychiatrist conducting the session was arrested and charged with manslaughter, fined and lost his medical license.

An example of the danger of concealment occurred in a group in the US, where one woman participant developed dissociative symptoms after a session with MDMA: she could intermittently not remember where she was or what she was doing, although she seemed not to be in distress and her vital signs, including pulse and temperature, were normal. When she was eventually admitted to a hospital it turned out that her sodium levels were radically depleted (*hyponatremia*) and she was close to death. She had ignored and lied about the explicit pre-cautionary requirement on antibiotics – and in fact had had major dental surgery a few days before and was on a heavy schedule of antibiotics. She did eventually recover her health, after her sodium-potassium balance was restored – but she never recovered a full memory of her experience, which had been more or less completely dissociated.

So the safest practice for self-organizing groups of entheogenic explorers would be to avoid all other psychoactive drugs, such as SSRIs and all antibiotics and anti-histamines for several days before and during the course of the experience. Even so, there is still a certain level of risk that comes from people, who either unknowingly or recklessly violate precautionary agreements.

Emergencies requiring outside intervention

There are two kinds of emergency situations that can arise for groups of entheogenic explorers – one where the emergency is caused by some event external to the group and one where a medical emergency arises within the group. Groups of entheogenic explorers are usually in a more or less concentrated trance state absorbed in inner exploration, though there may be one person in a leadership role who is more in contact with outer reality demands – which is one of the main reasons for having a non-ingesting co-facilitator.

I remember many years ago being with a group of psychedelic voyagers who were meeting in a place in the San Gabriel mountains, in the greater Los Angeles area. The area was (and still is) subject to frequent wild-fires in the dry season. On this occasion there had been wild-fires, but the area where we were meeting had been spared so far – though residents and visitors had been warned to be prepared for evacuation. Before our session started we discussed and mentally rehearsed what we would do if an evacuation order were to come. We agreed that we would intentionally close off further inner exploration, calmly gather and pack our personal effects into our cars and drive off. Having rehearsed and prepared we were able to focus on the processes for which we had assembled without any anticipatory anxiety. The firemen came and went and everything worked out smoothly.

For medical emergencies arising within the group, the trickiest aspect is recognizing when a situation arises that requires immediate outside intervention – or will resolve itself. In the situation described above, one person in the group was a trained paramedic – but even so could not recognize the symptoms of hyponatremia the woman was experiencing, which did not seem life-threatening. In retrospect, it would have been better to call an ambulance earlier. Sometimes also, when the use of illegal substances are involved, people are afraid of calling for medical help for fear of attracting police intervention. It has been my experience that emergency medical personnel, at least in the US, tend to be focused on doing whatever life-saving maneuvers need to be done, and do not generally concern themselves with law enforcement procedures.

For entheogenic explorers in the underground culture, who are taking powerful substances in a non-medical setting, I recommend paying explicit attention to medical emergency coverage, as a practice that ensures safety and reduces the anxiety of the travelers. Even in groups that contain one or more physicians as participants, it is best to have an explicit prior agreement with the MD that he or she is willing to step into the doctor role if called upon and making the judgment when outside intervention is necessary. (Again, since we are talking about an underground culture here, physicians may or may not be willing to assume such a risk).

If no physicians are in the group, an alternative is to ask a physician friend or acquaintance, preferably one who lives nearby, to be available for "on-call" consultation or even emergency visit. I have been in a situation where a person I was working with individually was exhibiting symptoms that I had trouble identifying, in reaction to a usually harmless substance. I called an osteopathic physician colleague, who suggested, over the phone, some easy pressure points I could use to help the person regain their biochemical equilibrium state – which they eventually did.

Sexuality and entheogens

As far as I know, the majority of the groups of entheogenic explorers adhere to a policy of no sexual activity during the ceremony – since it is seen as distracting from the main issues of healing and visioning and can bring a separative energy into the ceremony. The protocol that Sasha and Ann Shulgin developed for their research groups allows for married couples in the group to temporarily absent themselves to a separate room for sexual communication – but any other new pairings are avoided by prior agreement.

A central aspect of the classical consciousness-expanding psychedelic experience is the recognition of pre-imprinted familial and societal restrictions on thought, perception, feeling and behavior. This of course includes recognition of the accepted restrictions on the expression of sexuality – particularly in a culture as deeply imbued with puritanical values as the North American and European.

As Ram Dass and I relate in our memoir of the early 1960s era, *Birth of a Psychedelic Culture*, the issues of sexual activity and expressed or unexpressed sexual attraction in psychedelic experiences, with their enormous magnification of subtle bodily cues and signals, can very quickly lead to the disruption of group cohesiveness and even to the permanent alienation of life-long friendships or partnerships. Several examples of the unhappy consequences of non-attentive sexual attraction and activity are related in my books *Through the Gateway of the Heart*, *The Toad and the Jaguar*, as well as the anthologies on ayahuasca and on psilocybe mushroom experiences.

I recall a group session I facilitated in Switzerland in the mid-1970s, in which some of the participants were practitioners and teachers of a modern Tantric approach to sexuality. This approach eschews typical reproductive sexuality with the male ejaculation peak-orgasm, in favor of a slow, meditative, mindful exchange of intimacies that can involve prolonged orgasmic plateaus. The Tantra adherents in the group were inclined to challenge the view of indigenous cultures that sexuality involves a depletion of vital force and require fasting from both food and sexual activity both before and during the use of entheogenic plant substances. Perhaps, the Tantrikas suggested, this depletion of vital force only occurs with normal reproductive sex – but not with hyperconscious non-ejaculatory tantric sex.

Sexual behavior amplified by psychedelic drugs may of course play a role in mass celebratory events like Burning Man and other festivals. The mind-expanding potentials of sexuality enhanced by psychedelics have probably been explored by many and have also been described in writings such as *The New Science of Psychedelics*, by David Jay Brown. The issue is moot with the kinds of group rituals we are describing and considering here, since it is universally agreed that sexual behavior between couples should stay private and does not belong in group ceremonies with entheogens.

In therapist-guided individual sessions, the issue of sexual attraction arising within the session needs to be explicitly addressed, as it would and should be in any psychotherapeutic encounter, with or without entheogenic amplification. The empathic heart-opening characteristic of the typical MDMA experience has misled many insufficiently attentive individuals to make mistakes in judgment around intimacy behavior. However, as I point out in *Through the Gateway of the Heart*, the psychopharmacological action of MDMA in stimulating the release of prolactin and oxytocin, both hormones associated with non-sexual physical closeness and emotional intimacy – has introduced a benign safety feature into the therapeutic alliance, as well as into mass rave dance events. Simultaneously, it has led to the disruption of sexual exploitation maneuvers and considerable annoyance on the part of unscrupulous South American "shamans" who have found themselves unable to perform with their female Western acolytes on this accursed new drug.

Within the three Brazilian ayahuasca churches, attitudes toward sexuality and sensuality are predictably conservative – since they arose and exist within a mainstream culture dominated by the Catholic church. Western observer-participants in their church ceremonies, myself included, have nevertheless noticed some minor differences between the churches. In the ceremonies of the UDV, participants sit in straight-back chairs in a brightly-lit room and listen to sermons from the *Maistres*. These sermons tend to emphasize self-control of feelings and sexual behavior – which, to the Western observer aware of the enormous amplification of physical and sensuous feelings and sensations elicited by the plant substance, appears challenging in comparison to the self-control preached and expected in regular Christian churches.

Similarly challenging issues arise in the *Santo Daime* churches where at least physical expression of sensuality is permitted through the rhythmic movements of the structured dances. I have heard, through translations, the conductors of such ceremonies, exhort and demand from their acolytes that they keep their arms straight and their eyes downcast on their hymn book to avoid staring at the sensuous flowing dance movements of their female counterparts on the other side of the room.

Menstruation and the use of entheogens

The female menstrual blood flow is another topic that can elicit strongly divergent opinions in an area where traditional and indigenous mores intersect with modern sensibilities. Many (if not most) contemporary Westerners tend to dismiss the almost universal prohibition in indigenous cultures against women during their moon time participating in entheogenic ceremonies or indeed any ceremonies with men, as a primitive patriarchal taboo. This taboo tends to be interpreted as a relic of anti-female superstition. However, I once was in a mixed gender ritual circle in California where some radical feminists insisted on challenging traditional expectations by placing their menstrual pads on the altar in the middle of the circle. The distinctive though unspoken shock reaction in the group seemed to support the traditional practice of separate women's rites during menstruation.

While I have neither the knowledge nor the inclination to question the bio-psychological factors that may underlie such a prohibition, I have noticed that the average modern Westerner who becomes interested in indigenous practices with entheogenic plants, tends to automatically dismiss such ideas, which are regarded as culture-specific. As with the restricted diets traditionally associated with ayahuasca consumption I would rather assume first that perhaps there is a valid reason, based on accumulated experience, behind such seemingly irrational taboos – and then gather further observations relevant to the question.

I have made some observations which led me to question the automatic assumption that the menstrual taboo can be ignored in relationship to the intake of entheogens. In one group session one of the women, with a moderate degree of prior personal experience, when taking a moderate dose of mushrooms went into an extreme "spaced-out" state, where she felt only tenuously connected to the here-now reality of the group of fellow voyagers. In other words, during the menstrual period, her nervous system sensitivity and reactivity appeared to be enormously amplified.

My colleagues and I agreed at that time that it would be wise in future to mention this possibly complicating factor and recommend that women "on their moon," if they choose to take a psychedelic at all, consider taking a lower dose of the medicine than they would normally take.

The problem of over-idealization and grandiosity

This is a difficult issue to identify in oneself and to deal with when it occurs in others with whom you're related or interacting. Here's a typical scenario, that we experienced and observed many times at Millbrook, as Ram Dass and I related in *Birth of a Psychedelic Culture:* someone takes LSD or another psychedelic and has the most profound religious/spiritual/cosmic experience of their life, filled with deep insight into the mysteries of existence – and convinced it is their personal mission to bring this world-changing realization to the masses and to the world. Tim Leary, in one of his autobiographical books relates how Allen Ginsberg, sometime early in 1960, high on psilocybin as part of the Harvard projects, without his glasses or his clothes on, decided he had found the secret to world peace and insisted on trying to reach both J. F. Kennedy and Nikita Krushchev on the telephone right away to tell them of this discovery. Leary writes how he managed to persuade Allen to at least wait a few hours until his normal mode of consciousness had returned – which would take a few hours, but on occasion could take as long as a few days.

When we were living in an extended spiritual and research community at Millbrook and could provide a safe setting where autonomous psychedelic explorers could go on their trip, we would all too often experience someone re-appearing in the community from a psychedelic retreat space with a wild-eyed stare that said "I've found the deepest secret of the universe and need to share it, so people will recognize me for its profound significance." We would then ruefully roll our eyes and ask someone to keep an eye on the "lost in space" explorer to make sure he or she stayed physically safe. We would always encourage them to write it down or record it – so that whatever genuine insights were part of the mix could be saved for later evaluation and writing or recording.

It was abundantly clear also, that if and when such over-idealizing grandiosity occurred in an individual who did not have a supportive family or community – all bets were off for a successful integration. Some of the chaotic, life- and sanity-threatening experiences that have occurred with psychedelics and continue to occur at times in the underground psychedelic culture are largely due to the lack of preparation of set and setting, as well as purity and dosage of the various substances not being sufficiently carefully attended.

More subtle forms of over-idealization can also take the form of inner space explorers enthusiastically offering guided psychedelic trips to friends, relatives and others, based on their own truly authentic mystical or transformative experiences – and yet with insufficient knowledge and experience to navigate some of the trickier shoals and narrows that can unexpectedly occur in such intensive inner journeys. This is of course the reason why the MAPS and Heffter organizations and other researchers are developing training protocols for potential trip guides in the emerging new field of entheogenic psychotherapy and healing. This is also one of the basic reasons why I have chosen to write this book – to help inner space explorers, healers and spiritual seekers maximize their chances of finding the living truths and healing wisdom to which their soul aspires.

Four

Closing Ceremony and Integration

When we are asleep, we each live in our own world.
When we are awake, we all live in the one great world.

~Heraclitus

In our ordinary consciousness,
we each live in the personal reality of our own worldview.
When we awaken to higher consciousness,
we become aware of our place in the greater all-encompassing cosmos.

~Transcription by RM

There is a wide diversity in the amount of time and care given to post-session integration practices. Most of the circles I've been connected with and observed over the past thirty or forty years have adopted as a general practice to devote approximately equal amount of time and attention to preparation, the session itself and the integration afterwards. In a typical example, a group of friends might gather for a week-end, spend some hours socializing, preparing and sharing their intentions; then more formally sitting (or lying) in ceremony for several hours; and after a night's sleep, gather in the morning after breakfast to share descriptions and reflections on the inner journey and its applications in their life. Although Leary, Alpert and myself did emphasize, in our "psychedelic manual" based on *The Tibetan Book of the Dead*, the need and value of post-session integration as well as preparation, I cannot say that our practice always lived up to our ideals – and post-session integration was often left up to the individual.

We can review the integrative practices in the different kinds of sessions described in Part I.

(1) The psychedelic psychotherapy sessions in a medical clinic usually involve several non-drug psychotherapy sessions beforehand and thorough post-session follow-up. If the sessions are part of a research project they may also involve the subjects filling out personality tests before and after the session; and further tests and evaluative interviews at different longer intervals, like a month, 3 months and 6 months afterwards. Before and after personality assessments with questionnaires and interviews were also used in the Harvard psilocybin prisoner-rehabilitation projects of the early 1960s. The narcotic drug addiction treatment programs using ibogaine use varying degrees of post-session supportive treatment and assessments.

(2) The sessions held in non-psychiatric group meetings vary a great deal in the amount of pre-session preparation and post-session integration. The general presumption is that the participants in these session are not psychiatric patients receiving therapeutic interventions, but self-selected individuals taking full responsibility for their own inner processes and safety, in the protected company of like-minded individuals. In the research groups conducted by the Shulgins and described in their books *TIHKAL* and *PIHKAL*, there is a standard post-session follow-up that includes gathering information from the participants in the context of sharing and socializing.

(3) In traditional *NAC* peyote ceremonies, as far as one can tell from the descriptions, there is much less time devoted to post-session integration than to preparation. There is no telling of stories

or visions received – these are considered a private matter, possibly discussed only in the context of family. After a traditional all-night ceremony in a tepee, participants may gather in the morning to drink coffee and share a meal, chat and converse, possibly smoke a cigarette (not a ceremonial smoke) and then return to their families and lives.

Similar post-session practices apply in the traditional Mazatec mushroom sessions and the Amazonian *mestizo* ayahuasca ceremonies. The shaman or medicine person is a recognized professional healer who comes and conducts the healing ceremonies, with their songs and their medicines, at the end of which he or she goes home and is not otherwise involved. However in these small-scale indigenous communities the healer-shaman is usually known to the participants, or may even be a family member – so the integrative healing follow-up can take place within the family or the community. The situation is quite different for outside visitors from another culture, who will need to take responsibility for their own integrative processing.

This is an ongoing issue in the large number of ayahuasca ceremonies that are now conducted for Westerners, sometimes by traditional healers, sometimes by Westerners with varying degrees of knowledge and experience in conducting ayahuasca ceremonies. Furthermore, the North American and European participants generally do not have the community of family and friends who are familiar with and supportive of the healing journeys with indigenous medicine people. On the contrary, the families and medical professionals connected with present-day entheogenic explorers are just as likely to be alarmed or even antagonistic to Westerners seeking ayahuasca healing or visions. There is also likely to be minimal or no understanding by Westerners of the possible dangers of psychic attacks by healers on other healers, in which the psyches and sometimes even the lives of innocent Western participants can be at risk of unintentional "collateral damage." I had such an experience of being the victim of malicious sorcery myself – in which I ended up being hospitalized and evacuated from the Ecuadorian jungle with a case of dengue fever. I wrote up this story in an article in the magazine *Shaman's Drum*.

(4) In Brazil there exist three state-recognized religions that incorporate the taking of ayahuasca in their ceremonies – the *Uniao de Vegetal*, the *Santo Daime* and *Barquinia*. These religious movements exemplify a distinctly different paradigm for the use of the plant substances we have been discussing – not shamanic, not healing and not concerned with psychological insight or understanding. The closest Western equivalent to these ayahuasca churches might be something like American gospel ceremonies, with their hand-clapping and rhythmic chanting, or Quaker ceremonies with people speaking their inner truths. There is no interest in these church ceremonies for descriptions of inner experiences or encounters with spirits. If visions occur, they are not shared or discussed. I remember attending a UDV ceremony in Brazil and asking one of the participants afterwards what his experience was. He didn't understand my question – to him it was as inappropriate as asking someone coming out of a Sunday church ceremony about their "experience." Attending the ceremony was about community, devotion, faith, singing and prayer – not psychological insight or other-worldly visions.

Closing the circle and giving thanks

In contemporary neo-shamanic medicine circles, there is wide variation in the degree of attention given to post-session closing and integration – even when there is heightened awareness of the importance of preparation and intention. The closing ceremony ideally should mark the return to the ordinary time-space world, mirroring the opening ceremonial departure into non-ordinary space-time. My own appreciation of the importance of the post-journey integrative sharing was heightened when I participated in some of the vision quest workshops organized by the *School of Lost Borders*, founded by Steven Foster and Meredith Little. In these workshops the stimulus to heightened states of consciousness was not the ingestion of a psychoactive substance, but rather a water-only fasting and wilderness solitude experience for four days and nights. There were four days of preparatory training beforehand and about four days of integrative sharing afterwards. In the integration period each participant in turn was invited to tell the story of their inner journey when alone, and the guide's skillful questioning could assist them in integrating their findings into their ordinary lives of family and work.

I learned from these experiences that an initiatory journey, whether into an outer wilderness or into the hidden realms of the unknown psyche, needs to be followed by some kind of formal closing and an integrative round of story-telling to one's companions of family and community. If the experiential exploration is not followed by a process of intentional integration it is likely at best to be an isolated "trip" of some kind, or at worst it could lead to even deeper states of dislocation and alienation.

The consequences of a lack of attention to closing ceremony was brought home to me some years ago when I attended some ayahuasca ceremonies in Brazil organized by Western-trained anthropologists and psychologists. They had studied and participated in the indigenous ceremonies, but were not actually initiated in a traditional healing path, nor were they trained in psychotherapy practices. In those sessions there was an initial declaration of intention by the participants, and invocation of the guiding spirits – but there was no formal closing ceremony. After three to four hours from the initial intake, some participants chose to take an additional dose of the medicine and remain in the circle listening to music, some could choose to take an additional dose and go to their bedroom to be alone, some could go to another part of the house to eat and socialize. I suggested to the group leaders that it was better to have some kind of simple closing ceremony, clearly marking the beginning and ending of dedicated ritual time-space. Then some participants would and could disperse and gather socially, or some could still continue with their own inner journeying, preferably in a semi-separate quiet space.

The above example also illustrates the importance of prior agreement about supplemental dosing with the medicines. I have repeatedly experienced how difficult it is to have much of a meaningful closing ceremony if some people are still actively engaged in deep interior states, whereas some are mostly coming back to ordinary reality. This is also one of the criteria that distinguishes primarily recreational use of psychoactive substances, as distinct from self-selected groups of inner world explorers who agree on conditions of departure and return, and want to learn from each other's experiences as well as their own.

Explicitly bidding good-bye and giving thanks to both the incarnate human beings and discarnate spirits that guided and accompanied us on our journey is a practice as natural and obvious as saying thanks and good-bye to family and friends when we have shared a journey or participated in a gathering. Gratitude recognizes and affirms the continuity of the relationship and expresses good will and expectations for future shared explorations and companionship. The shamanic traditions know well the importance of invoking your particular power animals and guiding spirits at the beginning of a project or journey, and expressing gratitude and appreciation at the end.

The thanksgiving need not be an elaborate procedure, and it need not even be spoken. I have seen traditional shamans murmur their appreciation to their spirits while quietly scattering some tobacco or sage at a particular place we had gathered. Giving thanks at the end of ceremony mirrors the invocations of guiding spirits at the beginning. We affirm the value of the relationships we have with all the beings with whom we are connected, the human, the earthly-planetary and the spiritual-cosmic.

Just as we may start the ceremony by invoking the great cosmic-planetary spirits of the four directions and the time and the place, it is appropriate to offer a thanksgiving prayer, to affirm with gratitude our relationship with these planetary spirit beings. An example of such a thanksgiving prayer is given in the *Epilogue*. A final round of thanksgiving some groups use in ceremonies is to explicitly thank the companions who have shared the journey into deep inner spaces of healing and visioning. This affirms the spiritual connection each voyager has with fellow explorers, which may or may not also be a personal friendship, depending on how the circle was gathered together.

Conscious attention paid to the closing of a circle ceremony is as important as attending to the beginning. It is important to clearly and intentionally mark the transitions between ordinary and ritual time-space. The groups I have been involved with as participant-observer, have experimented with various kinds of closing ceremony, including the thanksgiving ritual described above.

One aspect of practice to consider with care and attentiveness is how much verbal description or story-telling of the journey one would do while still sitting in circle and before breaking up for eating and socializing. With the variable drawn-out endings typical of entheogenic experiences, some people in a group may still be in deep inner states, focused primarily in right-brain, non-verbal modes of awareness, while others are ready to move to a socializing mode. Some groups I have observed ask people to select and relate just one particular image, insight, or revelation from the journey that they value and will want to remember and contemplate further. Even this can prove to be quite strenuous and difficult, as people struggle to "translate" their non-verbal images and insights into verbal form – while still in touch with the deep, emotionally-charged experiences of the journey. There is really nothing to be gained by trying to prematurely force this kind of translation. It is probably most productive to let the experiences gradually be assimilated and integrated with overnight dreaming processes, and then be remembered and related the next day in the cool light of the ordinary reasoning mind.

Integration and the telling of stories

Recording and communicating one's experience afterwards, whether in written or pictorial form, or recording on an audio device, is as important as the intentional preparation beforehand. Our dreams and experiences only really become part of our ongoing growth and learning when recorded or told in some way. Mind-expanding drug experiences from which we don't remember any content, although they may be recreational and pleasurable and therefore appreciated for themselves, don't contribute much to our ongoing growth or self-understanding.

Outer world explorers of former times who discovered new lands and continents, like Christopher Columbus, Marco Polo or Alexander von Humboldt, made their contributions to contemporary society by describing and recording their discoveries. This may in fact be one of the criteria distinguishing the visions of discovery and creativity from the purely subjective hallucinations of madness. Are the visions communicated, whether in scientific or artistic images and symbols, or are they locked up in a private mind-space, without pointers that can lead others to repeat and extend the observations of the pioneers?

In regard to psychedelic substances, the historic accounts of their experiences by pioneering explorers of inner space like William James, Albert Hofmann, R. Gordon Wasson, Aldous Huxley, Stanislav Grof, Humphrey Osmond, Timothy Leary, Terence McKenna and many others have provided guides and maps for others eager to explore the expanded vistas of understanding and possibilities of healing afforded by these unusual substances. As my contribution to this shared scientific enterprise I have collected, edited and published four volumes of accounts of experiences with visionary plants, drugs and fungi – volumes that included descriptions of subjective experiences as well as summaries of the known science – botany, mycology, chemistry, pharmacology – of these substances.

The recording of experiences can be distinguished from its communication to others, although they are often connected. It can be a two-stage process, just as with dreams. The first step is to write down or record one's observations: what did I actually see or feel or experience? Just as with dreams, in recording or relating the entheogenic or psychedelic visions, it is a useful discipline, though not always easy, to clearly distinguish clearly between what I saw, felt and thought from my interpretations and associations of the psychological or philosophical meanings behind the experience. The use of an ongoing journal in which we describe all dreams and notes of observations in any and all states of consciousness is an extremely valuable practice.

A further aspect of integration is the sharing of the vision with others, the telling or writing of the story to a listening or reading audience. In group ceremonies, we are encouraged to relate something from our experience – what we saw and felt, and what we think about that and what we learned from it. There is, of necessity, a selective process involved here and even perhaps, creative and imaginative elaboration. We are in the shamanic borderlands between healing painful memories and envisioning inspiring futures.

It is part of the respect and mutuality of such group journeys of fellow explorers that no one is pressured into sharing what they don't feel comfortable to relate. (In psychedelic sessions that are part of an individual psychotherapy process, there are agreements of disclosure and privacy that are made explicit and respected.) Nevertheless, even within such agreed-upon constraints, for most of the people in the groups I've been involved with over the past forty years, it has been the near-universal experience that the participants learn an enormous amount by hearing the accounts of other travelers on a shared entheogenic journey.

The groups I have been in as participant-observer have usually also adopted the following practice from Council group circles, themselves based on Native American practices. When people relate their journeys and findings, the others listen with full attention but offer no interpretations or questions. Doing so could easily derail the process into pointless theoretical quibbles, comparisons or disagreements. The tone set by the leader in such situations is crucial to how this process works out.

At one point in the multi-year process of working out practical ground-rules for these integration rounds, I noticed that some people were making notes, or even recording on their laptops, while someone else was relating their experience. I realized there were two issues involved here: one was the possible threat to the confidentiality agreement – you do not want to even raise the possibility that someone else might be writing down aspects of your experience. The second issue was that if you're writing down your own notes, you're not really listening with full attention to the speaker or story-teller. The discomfort arising out of these two conflicts can be resolved by agreeing that there is no taking of notes when someone else is relating their experience. Instead everyone would pay full attention to the speaker.

Both the English phrase "pay attention" and the German equivalent "*schenk die Aufmerksamkeit*" make it clear that listening with attention is not just passive receiving but an active gift or payment. Attentive listening, without questioning but with compassion, functions in a sort of magnetic way to draw the story of the speaker's inner journey forth into verbal expression.

In the Grof *holotropic breathwork* sessions and other deep psychotherapeutic processes the integrative process occurs by way of the creation of a drawing or painting at the end of the experience.

C. G. Jung and his followers developed the use of mandala-drawing as well as tree-drawing for expressing the integrative processes in dreams or holotropic experiences. This practice can naturally also be extended to experiences with psychedelic substances. It seems likely that while verbal communications, whether spoken or written, engage the left-hemisphere language centers of the brain, drawing and painting engage the right-hemisphere imaginal functions. The two forms of expression communicate two quite different but complementary dimensions of our being and our experience.

Some say that movement and dance are additional non-verbal and non-graphic means of communicating one's experience and expressing – "bringing forth" – that which is within for others to see. While this is certainly true, the dance or movement mode of communication is ephemeral and does not leave a record, unless it is filmed. The same would be true of musical performance, whether instrumental or vocal, unless it is recorded. So it makes sense to distinguish the function of communicating one's experience for others, from the function of expressing it for one's own ongoing learning process. Both functions are important and deserve our attention and our intentional practice.

Celebration

At the end of our healing and visioning ceremony, our shamanic journeying, alchemical processing and yogic-meditative practicing, it is certainly appropriate and to be recommended that we move into celebration mode, with eating and drinking, possibly dancing, music and the fellowship of good humor and relaxed conversation. Even the old alchemists wrote in their treatises that the practitioner or student of the "art" should be sure to "unbend their mind" from time to time from its practice of concentration. Fasting before the work is balanced by feasting afterwards. It is one of the core Middle Way teachings of Gautama Buddha's life-story, that after practicing austerities for months, along with fellow ascetics, he finally accepted some milk to drink from a cow-herd maiden – turning away from an extremist path of self-deprivation and negation.

The place of entheogens in ongoing practice

In the introductory chapter I discussed the possible applications of entheogenic amplifiers and catalysts in methods of healing, explorations of consciousness, creativity enhancement and spiritual practice. I have chosen, in this book, not to discuss the use of psychedelic drugs in primarily recreational pursuits – such as rave dances or free-form tripping, even although that usage may be a greater or lesser part of the motivation of people ingesting these substances. Recreational use of a substance, almost by definition, does not really require a guidebook – though accurate information around the safety of particular substances is always to be recommended.

The frequency of use of entheogens and their integration, or lack thereof, into an ongoing life-style obviously varies enormously in the different use paradigms we have discussed. For participant subjects in the officially-approved medical research projects, the issue of repeated sessions, unless these are part of the research design, is moot. In fact, therapist-researchers have sometimes poignantly commented on the fact that subjects who have participated in one of their successful MDMA treatment-research sessions with trauma survivors, were not able to offer the subjects additional sessions, although safety and effectiveness had been amply demonstrated.

This therapists' dilemma is purely a consequence of the restrictions imposed, for political reasons, on physicians wanting to use medically proven though officially unapproved remedies.

In the *Native American Church* using peyote and the Brazilian churches using ayahuasca, which have the legal right to use their respective sacraments in their ceremonies, the frequency of use is determined by the organization and or its ceremonial calendar. With the *NAC* and its off-shoot peyote groups, there is usually an appeal to an elder to conduct a ceremony in response to an individual or family need. The Brazil-based *Santo Daime* churches have their regular weekly or monthly services, as well as special ceremonies on request. Traditional Mexican mushroom or South American ayahuasca ceremonies are generally held in response to a healing request by a member of the community – or, in contemporary conditions, by groups of tourists looking for an exotic experience.

In the ceremonies I have been calling hybrid shamanic-entheogenic, whether with a leader or self-directed, there is great variation in the frequency with which such ceremonies are organized. Sometimes a small group of friends and colleagues have an agreement to meet for ceremony regularly, perhaps once a year, or four times a year in the four seasons, or once a month – perhaps at the Full Moon for pagan-oriented groups. In some traditional societies and some contemporary groups, consciousness-altering substances have been used to mark the adolescent transition, from an identification as child to identification with the community of men or women. Sometimes such transition rites may also be organized along with sensory isolation or wilderness alone-time vision quest.

Individuals in contemporary Western urban cultures vary enormously in the frequency with which they ingest entheogens.

I have known individuals who chose to participate only once in a ceremony – perhaps to break through a block in creativity, or to work through a break-up of a relationship, or to signal a major life-transition in work – and then felt no further need or interest in further sessions. My old friend and colleague Ram Dass has said he chooses perhaps once a year to participate in an entheogenic session – just to tune in with his higher Self, to see if he is still in touch. Another old friend and mentor Alan Watts, who participated and advised our first projects at Harvard – used to joke "when you get the (cosmic) message, hang up the phone." Whether he felt he was expected to make some such cautionary statement, as a counter-culture spokesman, I do not know.

Those who choose to conduct healing ceremonies for others, or are in the process of learning how to do so, will have to consider their own individual life-trajectories and family-safety needs – determined by a complex mix of institutional and professional conditions – as well as the larger evolving socio-political context of the individual's "actually existing" nation-state. Those healers, explorers, artists and scientists interested in using these means in their practice with others and those who have chosen to become spokespersons and advocates for the integration of these tools into contemporary society will need to confront the pervasive but ignorant prohibitionist mind-set and police-state context of "drugs."

A few years ago, I was at one of the large international conferences of researchers and students in this field, held in Basel, Switzerland, traditional center of medieval alchemy. In the program mix of respected scientists, doctors, artists, philosophers and journalists – most of whom (perhaps all?) had experienced and were discussing the multiple properties and virtues of these new and yet ancient substances, there was an electrifying presentation by audio-tape from an individual who could, regrettably, not be present. It was a talk and an appeal by a young American, with no prior criminal background whatsoever, who had been arrested in England for possession of a quantity of LSD and hashish (no other drugs of any kind). No evidence was presented during his "trial" that any harm had been caused by his activity to anyone. He stated, in his defense, that his motive for making and distributing the sacrament was to contribute to societal improvement. For this he was serving a 20-year sentence, and had already lost one appeal.

The audio-taped statement was listened to by an audience of a couple of thousand people in respectful silence – focusing the following question in each listener: what does it mean that the maker and distributor of a substance which had been a sanity-saving remedy and/or an aid to enlightened understanding for many hundreds or perhaps thousands – was now "serving time" in jail? What kind of a society are we, that this is possible?

Books and References

Adamson, Sophia (aka Ralph Metzner) and Padma Catell, Editors (2012). *Through the Gateway of the Heart*. (2nd revised edition). Petaluma, CA: Solarium Press.

Brown, David Jay (2013). *The New Science of Psychedelics*. Rochester, VT: Park Street Press.

Callaway, J.C. Phytochemistry and Neuropharmacology of Ayahuasca. In: Metzner, Ralph, Editor (2014). *Ayahuasca - Sacred Vine of Spirits*. Rochester, VT: Park Street Press. (2nd edition).

Campbell, Don G. (1989). *The Roar of Silence. Healing Powers of Breath, Tone and Music*. Wheaton, Ill: Theosophical Publishing House.

Carhart-Harris, R.L., David Nutt, et. al. (2012) Neural correlates of the psychedelic state as determined by fMRI studies with psilocybin. *Proceedings of the National Academy of Sciences,* doi/10.1073/pnas.119598109.

Dass, Ram & Metzner, Ralph, with Bravo, Gary (2010). *Birth of a Psychedelic Culture*. Santa Fe, NM: Synergetic Press.

Foster, Steven & Little, Meredith (1989). *The Roaring of the Sacred River. The Wilderness Quest for Vision and Self-Healing*. NY: Prentice Hall Press.

Goldman, Jonathan (1998). *Shifting Frequencies*. Flagstaff, AZ: Light Technology Publishing.

Griffiths, Roland R., *et al.* (2006) Psilocybin can occasion mystical-type experiences having substantial and sustained personal meaning and spiritual significance. *Psychopharmacology.* Vol. 187 (3): 268-283.

Grob, Charles S., *et al.*(2011) A Pilot Study of Psilocybin Treatment for Anxiety in Patients with Advanced-Stage Cancer. *Arch Gen Psychiatry.* Vol. 68 (1): 71-78.

Grof, Stanislav & Grof, Christina (2010) *Holotropic Breathwork. A new approach to self-exploration and therapy*. Albany, NY: State University of New York Press.

Grof, Christina & Grof. Stanislav (1990). *The Stormy Search for Self. A guide to personal growth through transformational crisis*. Los Angeles, CA: Jeremy P. Tarcher.

Harner, Michael (2013). *Cave and Cosmos. Encounters with Another Reality.*

Berkeley, CA: North Atlantic Books.

Heaven, Ross (2013). *Shamanic Quest for the Spirit of Salvia*. Rochester, VT: Park Street Press.

Huxley, Aldous (1954). *The Doors of Perception*. New York: Harper.

Lee, Martin (2012). *Smoke Signals – A Social History of Marijuana – Medical, Recreational and Scientific*. New York: Scribner.

Luna, Luis Eduardo (1986). *Vegetalismo – Shamanism Among the Mestizo Population of the Peruvian Amazon*. Stockholm: Almqvist & Wiksell International.

Metzner, Ralph (1999). *Green Psychology*. With Foreword by Theodore Roszak and Epilogue by John Seed. Rochester, VT: Park Street Press.

Metzner, Ralph (2008). A Case of Ayahuasca Sorcery and Healing. In: *Shaman's Drum*, No. 77, pp. 42-46.

Metzner, Ralph (2009). *MindStates and TimeStream*. Berkeley, CA: Green Earth Foundation & Regent Press.

Metzner, Ralph (2012). *The Toad and the Jaguar*. Berkeley, CA: Green Earth Foundation & Regent Press.

Metzner, Ralph (2013). *Words Within and Worlds Beyond*. Berkeley, CA: Green Earth Foundation & Regent Press.

Metzner, Ralph & Leary, Timothy (1963) Hermann Hesse: Poet of the Interior Journey. *Psychedelic Review*, Issue #2, 167-182.

Metzner, Ralph, Editor (2014). *Ayahuasca - Sacred Vine of Spirits*. Rochester, VT: Park Street Press. (2nd edition).

Metzner, Ralph, Editor (2005). *Sacred Mushroom of Visions - Teonanácatl*. Rochester, VT: Park Street Press.

Nakkach, Silvia (2012). *Free Your Voice. Awaken to Life Through Singing*. Boulder, CO: Sounds True.

Naranjo, Claudio (1973). *The Healing Journey*. New York: Pantheon Books – Random House.

Oroc, James (2011) Psychedelics and Extreme Sports. in *Manifesting Minds*, edited by Rick Doblin and Brad Burge (MAPS). Berkeley, CA: Evolver Editions 2014.

Oss, O.T. & Oeric, O.N. (1976). *Psilocybin – Magic Mushroom Grower's Guide*. Berkeley, CA: AND/OR Press.

Ott, Jonathan (1994). *Ayahuasca Analogues*. Natural Products Co., Kennewick, WA.

Ott, Jonathan (1993). *Pharmacotheon*. Natural Products Co., Kennewick, WA.

Pahnke, W. N. and Richards, W. A. (1969). Implications of LSD and Experimental Mysticism. *J. Transpersonal Psychology*. Vol. I. No. 2, 69-102.

Passie, Torsten, *et. al.* (2005). "Ecstasy (MDMA) mimics the post-orgasmic state: Impairment of sexual drive and function due to acute MDMA-effects may be due to increased prolactin secretion." *Medical Hypotheses,* Vol. 64, 899-903.

Pendell, Dale (1995). *Pharmako/Poeia.* San Francisco, CA: Mercury House.

Pendell, Dale (2002). *Pharmako/Dynamis.* San Francisco, CA: Mercury House.

Pendell, Dale (2005). *Pharmako/Gnosis.* San Francisco, CA: Mercury House.

Penner, James, Editor (2014). *Timothy Leary – The Harvard Years. Early Writings on LSD and Psilocybin with Richard Alpert, Huston Smith, Ralph Metzner, and others.* Rochester, VT: Park Street Press.

Potter, Beverly and Joy, Dan (1998). *The Healing Magic of Cannabis.* Berkeley, CA: Ronin Publishing.

Presti, David E. and Nichols, David E. Biochemistry and Neuropharmacology of Psilocybin Mushrooms. In: Metzner, Ralph, Editor (2005). *Sacred Mushroom of Visions - Teonanácatl.* Rochester, VT: Park Street Press.

Richards, W., Rhead, J., DiLeo, F., Yensen, R. and Kurland, A. (1977) "The peak experience variable in DPT-assisted psychotherapy with cancer patients. *Journal of Psychedelic Drugs,* Vol. 9 (1), 1-10.

Roberts, Elizabeth & Amidon, Elias, Editors (1991). *Earth Prayers from Around the World.* HarperSanFranciso.

Seed, John & Macy, Joanna, and others (1988). *Thinking Like a Mountain: Toward a Council of All Beings.* Santa Cruz, CA: New Society Publishers.

Shulgin, Alexander & Shulgin Ann (1997). *TIHKAL – The Continuation.* Berkeley, CA: Transform Press.

Shulgin, Alexander & Shulgin Ann (1991). *PIHKAL – A Chemical Love Story.* Berkeley, CA: Transform Press.

Siebert, Daniel. *Divine Sage* (a comprehensive guide to *salvia divinorum*, work in progress). www.sagewisdom.org.

Stamets, Paul (1996). *Psilocybin Mushrooms of the World.* Berkeley, CA: Ten Speed Press.

Stolaroff, Myron (1997). *The Secret Chief.* Charlotte, NC: MAPS Publications.

Strassman, Rick (2000). *DMT: The Spirit Molecule.* Rochester, VT: Park Street Press.

Tart, Charles (1991). Influence of Previous Psychedelic Drug Experiences on Students of Tibetan Mysticism: A Preliminary Observation. *Journal of Transpersonal Psychology,* Vol. 23, No. 2, 139-176.

Trachsel, Daniel (2011). *Psychedelische Chemie.* Solothurn, Switzerland: Nachtschatten Verlag.

Trout, K & Friends (2005). *Trout's Notes on San Pedro & Related Trichocereus Species*. Mydriatic Productions.

Yatra da Silveira Barbosa (1998). Jurema Ritual in Northern Brazil. *MAPS Newsletter*, Vol. 8, No. 3.

Zimmerman, Jack & Coyle, Virginia (1996). *The Way of Council*, Las Vegas, NV: Bramble Books.

Epilogue

Four Elements Medicine Wheel Prayer

O Great Spirit of the East
Radiance of the rising Sun
Spirit of new beginnings
O Grandfather Fire
Great nuclear fire of the Sun.
Life-energy, vital spark,
Here is the power to see far,
And to envision with boldness,
To purify our senses, and
To awaken our hearts and our minds.

We pray that we may be aligned with you,
So that your energy may flow through us,
And be expressed by us,
For the good of this planet Earth,
And all sentient beings upon it.

O Great Spirit of the South
Protector of the fruitful land
And of all green and growing things,
O Grandmother Earth, Soul of Nature.
Here is the great power of the receptive,
Of nurturance and endurance,
Of growing and bringing forth,
The noble trees and grasses,
Fragrant flowers of the field,
Sweet fruits of the garden.

We pray that we may be aligned with you,
So that your power may flow through us,
And be expressed by us,
For the good of this planet Earth,
And all sentient beings upon it.

O Great Spirit of the West
Spirit of the deep waters,
Of rain and rivers, lakes and springs.
O Grandmother Ocean,
Fathomless womb of all life.
Here is the power to dissolve boundaries,
And release painful holdings,
To taste and to feel,
To cleanse and to heal,
Great blissful darkness of peace.

We pray that we may be aligned with you,
So that your power may flow through us,
And be expressed by us,
For the good of this planet Earth,
And all sentient beings upon it.

O Great Spirit of the North
Invisible Spirit of the Air,
And of the fresh, cool winds,
O vast and boundless Grandfather Sky,
Your living breath animates all life.
Here is the power of clarity and strength,
Sweeping out old forms and patterns,
Bringing change and challenge,
Opening to hear the voice of Spirit,
The ecstasy of movement and the dance.

We pray that we may be aligned with you,
So that your power may flow through us,
And be expressed by us,
For the good of this planet Earth,
And all sentient beings upon it.

Invocation of All the Spirits of Great Nature

We call upon the **Spirits of the Four Directions.**

Great Spirit of the East, O Grandfather Fire, the dawning of new vision,
Fiery warmth and vital spark, of inspiration and enthusiasm.

Great Spirit of the South, O Grandmother Earth, bringer of new life,
All green and growing things, receptive and nurturing, the fruitful land.

Great Spirit of the West, O Grandmother Ocean, of rivers, rain, lakes and
Springs, the depths of the ocean, place of dissolving, of healing and peace.

Great Spirit of the North, O Grandfather Sky, power of the great winds,
Sweeping out the old, bringing change and movement, clarity and strength.

May we be aligned and harmonized with them,
In our lives and our actions, in body, speech and mind.
We ask this for ourselves, all our relations, and all sentient beings.

We call upon the **Spirits of this Place**

The guardian spirits of this particular place,
This house and this region,
Its landforms and waterways,
Its elemental forces and energies,
Its fields and forests, plants and animals,
The two-legged humans of times past and present,
The natives and the dwellers.

We approach them with respect and appreciation,
Mindful of our interdependence,
The continuing balance of giving and receiving.

Note: In invoking the spirits of a particular place it is natural and appropriate to name and identify the specific geographic, ecological and cultural features of the particular place, which constitute in combination the *genius loci.* The wording given here is merely suggestive and specific names should be added or substituted.

We attune and harmonize with the **Spirits of the Cycles of Time**

The circadian cycle of the turning Earth,
Through morning dawn and noonday Sun,
Evening twilight and midnight darkness.

The monthly cycle of the Moon,
Phase of increase to Full Moon,
Time of flowing tides and growing plants;
Phase of decrease to Dark Moon,
Time of radiant stars and deeper space.

The seasonal cycle of Sun and Earth,
Through Spring and through Fall, the great cosmic doorways of Equinox;
Through Summer and Winter, the great cosmic doorways of Solstice.

The ever-changing cycles of the Planets,
Held together in the gravitational embrace of the Sun,
Orbiting in ever-changing relationships to our life here on Earth.

Note: Here too, the wording given is only suggestive and the specific temporal phases of the diurnal, lunar and annual cycles should be named for attunement.

We call upon the **Spirits of the Animals**

Allies, guides, guardians, teachers, familiars, totems,
Compassionate companions on the Earth path –

The four-legged mammals, roaming the lands of the Earth;
The winged and far-seeing spirits of air, soaring on the winds;
The swimming and diving spirits of water, gliding in the depths of the sea;
The crawling reptilian and amphibian,
At earth's surface and water's edge;
The tiny and delicate beings of the insect world.

We call upon them with respect and appreciation,
Honoring their wildness and their integrity,
Always mindful of our mutuality, the flowing balance
Of giving and receiving, receiving and giving.

We call upon the Spirits of the **Plants and the Fungi**

Remembering our biospheric symbiosis,
Cellular webs and mycelial networks of interdependence,
With roots and bark, seeds and spores, flowers and fungi.
Those providing substance and sustenance of food;
Those healing sickness and relieving pain;
Those delighting our senses and souls
With beauty of color and flowering fragrance.

And the plant teachers, vines of visions, herbs of healing,
Mushrooms of magic, ergot mother grains—
Gate-keepers and door openers to the spirit world.
Helping us cleanse the lenses of perception,
Helping us know our place in the great Web of Life.

We call upon them with respect and appreciation,
always mindful of our mutuality, the flowing balance
of receiving and giving, giving and receiving.

We call upon the **Spirits of the Mineral World**

Remembering the masters of rock and of stone,
The still ones of mountains and canyons;
The solid, enduring, primal, material.
The forms and foundations of buildings and bodies;
The mineral mothers of metals, of tools and machines,
Ornaments, armaments, instruments and implements.

The precious and beautiful jewels and gems,
Inspiring our senses with their radiance and color;
And the mineral matrix of glass and crystal,
Transparent, translucent, solidified light.

We honor these spirits of minerals and stones,
Respecting their autonomy and integrity,
Mindful of our mutuality,
And intimate interconnectedness.

We call upon the **Spirits of the Ancestors and Elders**

Remembering the names of our grandmothers and grandfathers,
We honor our familial forebears,
All those who have traveled before us
On the roads of living and dying,
With whom we are linked by genetic inheritance.
Who have passed on the thread of life
Through the generations,
To us and our children and descendants.
We thank you and ask for your blessings
On our lives and our journeys.

Remembering the names of our elders and teachers,
We honor the Wise Ones, the lineage holders,
Of former times and present days.
The sages and saints, gurus and guides,
Way-showers and master teachers,
Whose life wisdom and vision inspire us.
We thank you and ask for your blessings
On our lives and our journeys.

We call upon the **Spirits of our Human Relations**

Remembering the web of human interrelatedness,
The network of named relations,
The family relatives and the chosen affinities.

Calling the names and honoring the relations,
With the nearest and dearest,
The brothers and sisters, mothers and fathers,
The sons and daughters, partners and lovers,
Soul mates and heart friends,
Colleagues, associates, collaborators,
Co-conspirators in the human adventure,
Fellow travellers on this great Earth journey.

We affirm and appreciate our interrelatedness,
Ever mindful of our mutuality,
Respectful of our reciprocity.

We call upon the **Light-Beings of the Higher Realms**

Remembering the names of the archetypal Immortals,
Honoring these ancestors of peoples and cultures,
Ascended Masters, Spirit Guides, Ancient Ones,
Divine counselors of collective consciousness and culture.
Those living in higher dimensions of this Sun-Earth world,
And those who are visitors from other worlds and stars beyond,
Guiding our destinies from the spiritual realms.
Creator Deities, Great Cosmic Beings of Light.

We thank you for your inspiration,
And ask for your blessings
On our lives, our journeys and our world.

Giving Thanks to the Four Great Planetary Spirits

We thank you Grandfather Fire – who gives us Warmth

We thank you Grandmother Ocean – who brings us Peace

We thank you Grandfather Air – who brings us Change

We thank you Grandmother Earth – who gives us Life.

Green Earth Foundation
Harmonizing Humanity with Earth and Spirit

The Green Earth Foundation is an educational and research organization dedicated to the healing and harmonizing of the relationships between humanity and the Earth, through a recognition of the energetic and spiritual interconnectedness of all life-forms in all worlds. Our strategic objectives are to help bring about changes in attitudes, values, perceptions, and worldviews that are based on ecological balance and respect for the integrity of all life. Our areas of research interest include consciousness studies, shamanism and Earth mythology, and green and eco-psychology. Green Earth Foundation has produced and co-published a series of seven books by Ralph Metzner, Ph.D.

THE ECOLOGY OF CONSCIOUSNESS

1. The Expansion of Consciousness
2. The Roots of War and Domination
3. Alchemical Divination
4. MindSpace and TimeStream
5. The Life Cycle of the Human Soul
6. The Six Pathways of Destiny
7. Worlds Within and Worlds Beyond

See www.greenearthfound.org for other publications and projects, including newsletters and blogs by Ralph Metzner. The Green Earth Foundation is a 501(c)(3) non-profit, educational and research organization.

CPSIA information can be obtained
at www.ICGtesting.com
Printed in the USA
BVOW08s0804030118
504353BV00002B/193/P